MARGARITA

in

RETROGRADE

COCKTAILS for EVERY SIGN

VANESSA LI AND BOWEN GOH

ABRAMS IMAGE, NEW YORK

ASTROLOGICAL COCKTAILS

⭐⭐⭐⭐⭐

ARIES

TAURUS

GEMINI

CANCER

LEO

VIRGO

WHAT'S YOUR SIGN?

Although this question is well known as a cliché, three-tequila-sodas in, let-me-waste-your-time-because-you-clearly-have-so-much-of-it line when trying to pick up an attractive stranger at a bar, these days many of us find that astrological signs—ours, our friends', our crushes'—come up in conversation after conversation in our social and dating lives. Now that we're able to connect with so many more strangers than before with a casual slide in the DMs or just by Googling "bars that have pickleback shots" (nasty, but okay, we love them too), it's useful to be able to get the rundown on a new acquaintance using this shorthand without needing to spend ten thousand hours with them.

We are Vanessa (Scorpio Sun, Scorpio Moon, Aries Rising) and Bowen (Gemini Sun, Pisces Moon, Gemini Rising), best friends of almost a decade and bar co-owners. And while our function as a business is to sell drinks, our greatest joy is seeing the connections people make right in front of us, whether it's by sharing a love of music, creating meaningful relationships (how hot is friendship), or swapping saliva in a Danielle Steel–style embrace but instead of a windswept cliffside or horse stable, it's Brooklyn, baby.

In 2017, when we opened Mood Ring, a humble neighborhood bar in Bushwick, one of our main goals was to create a space where our guests could really mingle and let out their freakier side if they wanted to. As we designed Mood Ring's physical footprint, which contains a plush cocktail bar in front, a dance floor in the back, and a hallway of bathrooms connecting them, we were conscious that spatial tightness in strategic places creates the possibility of meaningful interactions. It's the idea that if you bump into a stranger, whether literally or just through eye contact, you can make a connection. And while the bathroom line can be long, it's also where we've seen friendships and relationships start.

We also believed that we could create the possibility of new interactions by taking inspiration from astrology. In our teenage years, astrology drove our understanding of the people around us—it could make or break a crush and explain why certain friendships lasted while others didn't—and it has never lost its power over us. As we got older, the connection between astrology and cocktails became clear to us, too. We would go out and grab drinks, celebrate birthdays with friends, meet strangers, and all the clashes or bonds between personalities from the night could be traced to the alliance between astrology and liquor. When we opened the bar, "What's your sign?" became our slogan (and WiFi password), and our main attraction was our astrology special, a rotating monthly cocktail that celebrates every astrological sign by using ingredients that play off each sign's unique characteristics and traits.

The schedule offers each sign the chance to shine and be the center of attention during their season. After a food-and-beverage blog erroneously posted that we offered all twelve astrology cocktails year-round, we spent months correcting the misinformation with customers who were upset to learn that they would have to wait months to taste their sign's drink. (And if there's one thing we've learned about the signs, it's that the one who really doesn't want to wait for their season is a Leo.) But your birthday is the day we get to celebrate you with your best friends—why not make it even more special?

The other benefit of a rotating menu is that it allows us to batch or stock unique and fresh ingredients that would be out of place at different times of year. People in the food world emphasize seasonal cooking all the time; this is our homage to that, but for drinks, and with an astrological twist.

We are often asked how we pick which ingredients are used for a specific sign. The easiest answer is that we choose by feeling, not logic. Our team, which has remained small throughout the years, is made up of similarly devoted astrology enthusiasts. Two of our bartenders, Randall Morris (Aries) and Sarah Rosenblatt (Virgo), have often taken the lead on crafting our astrology specials. As a team, we might choose to center the recipe around a base spirit—pepper-infused tequila for energetic and eccentric Aquarius, for example—or an ingredient we're excited by—like matcha for stable and chill Taurus—before choosing ingredients that would pair well with it. We also don't shy away from bringing in fun and silly elements. You probably would never see gummy bears listed as an ingredient at your typical cocktail bar, but we think two of them ass to ass on a skewer serve as the perfect garnish for a Gemini-twin cocktail.

Our intention for the cocktails in this book was to make them match their signs while being tasty and unique, and to finally give people with a range of budgets and skill sets the ability to make any of these cocktails whenever the mood strikes. For example, a number of our recipes feature Tito's vodka, not necessarily because we think it's he absolute best vodka in the world but because we think it's a solid choice that you can find at any liquor store and it comes with an affordable price tag.

The way this book is structured is that we will give a little introduction to each sign and what makes them special. After that you'll find the recipes we've created to match with that sign's season. And finally, at the end of each chapter are some helpful nightlife tips and tales tailor-made for that sign.

We see astrology as an incredible way to get to know someone because when you take all of the characteristics of someone's personality together—many of which may clash—you get a great view into who they really are. Mood Ring is the same way: we've combined all the things we loved and thrown them at the wall, and what's stuck shows you what we are about. Astrology, Hong Kong director Wong Kar-wai minimalist photography, acupressure machinery, bunnies, and Rainforest Cafe are influences that never belong in the same sentence, but somehow they've come together at Mood Ring, and it works. And with so many sources of inspiration, everyone can pick what they gravitate toward or which decorations they sneak into their bags—they can find the piece they like about the bar, just like we all find the things we like about each other, even if it's just our Rising signs.

Our staff has seen so much since we opened in September 2017. Relationships have bloomed after first dates under the red lights at Mood Ring, Gen Z adultery has unfolded in front of our eyes, breakups have ended with tears, and yes, we have caught a number of people having sex in the bathroom. Even now, we regularly hear some iteration of "Mood Ring? I love you guys—I fell in love for three weeks because of you." From the start, we have always hoped that we could create a space that made people feel welcome to be themselves. We are inspired by that feeling after you've had a drink or two and are feeling the chemistry with a new person—that feeling of hope and possibility. With the recipes and tips in this book, we think you'll be able to re-create a little bit of that magic wherever you are.

And even if we don't manage to get you laid—the cocktails aren't half bad.

So, What *Is* Your Sign?

If your date has ever asked you for your date and time of birth, it's because they want to dig into your full birth chart. They need to know if you're the kind of person they could be compatible enough with to share a one-bedroom apartment or more suited to that fleeting "your place or mine?" one-night stand. So yes, this is your permission slip to call your mom at 1 A.M. on a Saturday night to ask the million-dollar question: Hey, Mom, do you know where my birth certificate is?

Just knowing your Sun placement isn't enough to really get to know you and determine your potential compatibility, and we would take it as a lukewarm hint if a potential romantic interest were into astrology but didn't ask for the full lowdown on our chart. Nowadays you can quickly generate your full birth chart with apps like Co-Star and The Pattern, as long as you know your date, time, and place of birth. They also conveniently have social features that enable you to compare charts with your friends or crushes or—let's be honest—the massive football field–sized center of the Venn diagram between your friends and your crushes, aka your friends you have crushes on.

Together, your Sun, Moon, and Rising (or Ascendant) signs compose what many think of as the "trifecta" of your personality. While the Sun sign is the most frequently discussed sign, we like to remember that the other two are equally important (what would the Powerpuff Girls be without Bubbles and Buttercup?). There are many other illuminating placements you'll also see when you look at your entire birth chart, but you can start by looking at the big three.

Your Sun sign represents what you shine into the world—how you process everything around you. It reveals your most basic tendencies, so it is the sign people are most self-aware of. (It's also the simplest to calculate since you only need to know your birthday. The date ranges for each Sun sign can vary from source to source, but in this book we defer to the website Astrology Zone by Susan Miller, which we obsessively frequented during high school.) In general, your life's decisions and preoccupations reflect the inclinations of this sign. If you're a Scorpio, for example, you can't help but be passionate, brooding, and frankly very sexy. It's your unique aura—your glow.

Digging a bit deeper, your Moon sign represents your emotional self and the subconscious, or the soul of who you are. You can think of this as your internal self—who you are when you are alone or with the people closest to you. It's the difference between downing Margaritas at a crowded bar (Sun sign) and the after party at your apartment in your pajamas with your best friend drinking Merlot out of a cereal bowl you dug out of your cabinet (Moon sign).

Finally, your Rising sign is the "as above, so below" aspect of who you are. It's the micro reflecting in the macro, or how you present yourself to the world through everything you do, from your fashion choices to your everyday vernacular. Steve Jobs's Rising sign was the black turtleneck and blue jeans combo. Understanding the way you approach the people and world around you is vitally important to understand your whole self.

Our birth charts are complex because—get this—each of us is complex as hell. This is one of the reasons astrology is so fun! It can help us ask questions about ourselves, reflect, and conceive of unique ways to not only solve our problems but also understand why our problems are problems in the first place. It helps explain interpersonal relationships, and maybe why you can be a calm and sweet, indoor-voice-type person but still love your one loud Aquarius friend who gets kicked out of the club for stomping their ten-pound Dr. Martens on the custom reclaimed wood tables.

When it comes to drinking based on your sign, you'll likely be most excited about starting with your Sun sign. Just as astrology isn't black or white, neither is figuring out what all Libras or Aries might like to drink. Cocktail recipes can always be experimented with and certain ingredients substituted to your liking. For example, if you're someone who just simply does not enjoy drinking gin because you studied abroad one year, got drunk on gin, vomited in the hotel lobby, lost your passport, and had to spend the rest of the trip in a hostel with an odd stench while you waited for the embassy to come through, you can try swapping out the base liquor in any particular cocktail—just understand that you may have to do some trial and error if the other ingredients don't complement it perfectly.

We have concocted delicious offerings for every sign, and it's important not to limit yourself only to the cocktails in your Sun sign's section. Have fun with the other placements in your chart (why not try the cocktails from your Venus placement's section during Valentine's Day?), or celebrate whichever sign whose season we currently happen to be in. Let the world be your oyster.

Your Home Bar

We know that creating a home bar from scratch can be daunting, especially if you are new to making cocktails. We can demystify that for you! At the end of the day, we're all just trying to get drunk in the tastiest way possible.

     If you're like us, you don't like having a bunch of things sitting in your kitchen that you rarely use. So we'll start with the basics of what you'll need to make a good cocktail:

shaker

mixing
glass

jigger

strainer

barspoon

ice

SHAKER

There are different types of shakers, but the one we like using the most is the tin-on-tin Boston shaker: a pair of tins, one smaller and one larger.

Just like any other kitchen tool, you can find expensive designer versions, but there aren't many practical reasons to spend that much (but no shame if you just want something pretty on your bar cart!). We have a ton of shaker sets that cost $10–$15 and they can take a lot of use from the thousands of cocktails we make in a month. We treat them as delicately as your drunk ass treats your cellphone when you get home after a long night and chuck it across the room. For a good and affordable at-home option, we like the tin shaker set from Koriko, which retails for about $20.

NOTE **If the recipe says to shake a drink, it's important! You'll find that in cocktails with any juices, the drink needs to be shaken to achieve the proper texture and marry of all the ingredients. If you find yourself stuck at a friend's house without all the tools, feel free to do what you can with a little bit of resourcefulness. A mason jar can be your DIY shaker.**

STRAINER

You'll need a Hawthorne strainer, which is particularly good for shaken drinks. Cocktailian bartenders would recommend you get a separate Julep strainer to use for stirred drinks, but for convenience's sake, a lot of bars use the Hawthorne for both.

MIXING GLASS

This is a glass you'll use for any stirred cocktails. We recommend buying a tempered mixing glass because sudden temperature changes, such as washing a glass with warm or hot water and then putting ice in it immediately, can shatter the glass if it's not tempered.

NOTE **It's totally fine to use a shaker tin to stir your cocktails, but if you don't have a ton of experience making drinks, it's nice to be able to see what you're doing in a glass.**

BAR SPOON

You'll use this to stir cocktails in your mixing glass. Bar spoons have spiraled handles, which make them easier to control while stirring drinks. To stir a drink properly, the back of the spoon should always maintain contact with the walls of the mixing glass. If you're doing it right, the motion should come purely from your fingers, not your wrist. We also recommend pouring all the ingredients into the mixing glass before adding ice to minimize any splash back.

JIGGER

If you've ever sat at a bar and marveled at the bartender's ability to free-pour multiple drinks at a time, you're not alone. Free-pouring is a skill that takes time and practice to learn, but it makes sense when you're working behind the bar and trying to maximize the number of orders (and tips!) you can make. Still, there are establishments where bartenders are required to use jiggers for accuracy and precision. For the home bartender, they are a must. The measurements vary from model to model, but we've gotten accustomed to using a combined 1-ounce (30-ml) and 1½-ounce (45-ml) jigger. In our cocktails, we generally consider 1½ ounces (45 ml) to be a standard shot. You can buy different sizes; just make sure you know what measurements you're using.

Many cocktails will ask for ½ ounce (15 ml) or even ¼ ounce (8 ml) of an ingredient—if you're interested in being precise with your pours, look for a Japanese-style jigger that features etched lines demarcating these smaller amounts. Otherwise, you can eyeball it (i.e., fill about half of the 1-ounce/30-ml jigger for a ½-ounce/15-ml pour).

NOTE If you do decide to practice free-pouring and opt to put speed pourers on your home bottles, make sure to also buy pourer caps. Without them, anything from dust to fruit flies will find its way into your precious liquor, especially the sweeter ones.

ICE

If you plan on making cocktails for your own at-home enjoyment, you deserve to have some nice ice trays. We like keeping a few silicone ice trays with small- to medium-size square molds in our freezer. Square ice is ideal to work with for most of the cocktails you'll see in this book, and it's pretty, too.

There are times when we have to use less than ideal ice, like if we're having a bunch of people over or making drinks in an outdoor setting. Having to use convenience store ice cubes in the shape of frozen dinosaur chicken nuggets is annoying, but not the end of the world. If you have to buy a bag from a grocery store, try to look for one where the ice hasn't melted and reformed into huge chunks of ice. We like ice that has integrity and some sort of shape. As we learned from our high school physics class: the smaller the ice cubes, the larger the surface area per cube (for same volume of ice), and the faster the ice melts, the more watery your cocktail becomes.

NOTE The ice in your freezer absorbs odors and flavors from other items in the freezer. If you have a tray that's been sitting there for months, we recommend dumping the ice and washing the tray before reusing it. If your ice smells like frozen peas or sirloin steak, we definitely recommend throwing out the ice tartare and starting a new tray.

Glassware We Recommend

ROCKS GLASS

A short glass used to serve spirits neat or on the rocks, and we think of it as the most important and basic glass to have. Classic cocktails such as your Old Fashioned and Negroni are served in rocks glasses.

WINE GLASS

This is an entire category on its own, as you'll realize if you ever end up on the wine-nerd side of the internet like we have. For cocktails, we like using a particularly bulbous-shaped wine glass for our spritzes.

COUPE

A stemmed glass used to serve drinks "up," or without ice. You've seen this glass used for your Martinis (when the classic V-shaped Martini glass isn't available) and Manhattans served "up." We like using coupes for any cocktails where we really don't want the drink to be further diluted by ice over time, and also any cocktails with egg whites.

HIGHBALL

A long and narrow glass. If you order a "highball" drink at a bar (e.g., a tequila soda or gin & tonic), it'll likely come in one of these glasses, as the shape helps preserve the carbonation from the soda.

NICK & NORA

Another stemmed glass similar to the coupe but arguably more beautiful and elegant. These glasses typically run slightly smaller in size than the coupe, so if a cocktail uses particularly expensive or potent ingredients, we might opt to serve it in a Nick & Nora glass.

rocks   wine glass   coupe   highball   Nick & Nora

ASTROLOGICAL COCKTAILS

ARIES

MARCH 21–APRIL 19

A natural-born leader, the fiery Aries is courageous and bold enough to say what everyone else is thinking. We love you because you take the initiative to make things happen. When your sights are set on something, you lead with passion and will do everything in your power to achieve it. Let's just say Arieses make unforgettable scratch-marks-on-the-back lovers, and you're the ones at 6 A.M. high-fiving morning joggers on your way home from the club. You are also known for your mood swings and stubbornness, so when others say they want passion, they shouldn't forget that it can go both ways.

As an Aries on a date, you like to take the lead. You'll probably have an amazing go-to drink to recommend and can figure out a great plan for the rest of the night, whether it's drunkenly peeing and then jumping into trash cans (yes, we've seen it) or going to the underground rave you find by talking to a guy standing by the train tracks who gives you the address to a warehouse where the circus acrobats train. Aries love freedom and riding in cars with their head out the window, wind blasting, because they're not scared of much.

Our lead bartender, Randall Morris, is Mood Ring's resident Aries. He created two delicious cocktails included here for his birth season, the Dial 666 and the Firestarter.

IDEAL DATE
for an ARIES

You get on a bus with your date and sneak sips from a flask. All of a sudden, there's a bomb on the bus and you have to stay above 50 miles per hour on the highway or it'll blow. Your date looks at you and says, "*Wow, this is high stakes.*" Hot. You wink, and with one bead of sweat dripping down your temple, you disarm the bomb and save everyone on the bus. You end up making out with your date on the airplane tarmac with a few nicks here and there. Yes this is also the plot to *Speed* (1994), starring Keanu Reeves and Sandra Bullock, but let's get on that bus.

♡ EARTH, WIND & FIRE, "Devotion"

♡ GALAXY 2 GALAXY, "Jupiter Jazz"

♡ BAKAR, "Hell N Back"

♡ NINE INCH NAILS, "The Hand That Feeds"

♡ TRICKY, "Hell Is Round the Corner"

♡ NINES, "Oh My"

♡ THE CLASH, "Straight to Hell"

♡ JENEVIEVE, "Baby Powder"

♡ NATALIA LAFOURCADE, "Hasta la Raíz"

♡ MADISON AVENUE, "Don't Call Me Baby"

OUR ARIES PLAYLIST

Dial 666

★ ★ ★

This is the *glou-glou*, aka glug-glug, aka so-good-you'll-want-to-shotgun of cocktails. We believe that even an Aries's greatest hater couldn't help but love drinking this. The mezcal gives it a smoky base, and it's livened up by the sweetness of the passion-fruit juice. We also love the extra bite that comes from the Luxardo Maraschino liqueur.

GLASS TYPE

[ROCKS]

INGREDIENTS

1½ ounces (45 ml) Mezcal Union Uno

¼ ounce (8 ml) Luxardo Maraschino liqueur

1½ ounces (45 ml) passion-fruit juice

½ ounce (15 ml) lemon juice

Thyme sprig for garnish

DIRECTIONS

1. Pour the Mezcal Union Uno, Luxardo Maraschino, passion-fruit juice, and lemon juice into a cocktail shaker.

2. Add ice and shake vigorously.

3. Strain into a rocks glass filled with ice.

4. Garnish with the thyme sprig.

Eyes Without a Face

★ ★ ★

Aries, we know that it's exhausting yelling at people all day and sleeping with them at night. To go along with those evenings when you want a strong nightcap, this is what we recommend: a pleasant bourbon cocktail that will help you get the warm buzz you've been craving. Here we use Bib & Tucker bourbon, but if you're looking for something at a lower price point, we think Evan Williams Black Label is the best budget bourbon.

GLASS TYPE

[COUPE] or
[NICK & NORA]

INGREDIENTS

2 ounces (60 ml) Bib & Tucker bourbon

½ ounce (15 ml) American Fruits Apple Liqueur

½ ounce (15 ml) Dolin sweet vermouth

½ ounce (15 ml) simple syrup (instructions follow)

2 dashes Fee Brothers cardamom bitters

Maraschino cherry for garnish

recipe continues

DIRECTIONS

1. Pour the Bib & Tucker, American Fruits, Dolin, simple syrup, and Fee Brothers into a mixing glass.

2. Add ice to fill the mixing glass about halfway and stir with a bar spoon.

3. Strain into a chilled coupe or Nick & Nora glass.

4. Drop in a maraschino cherry for garnish.

 MAKING SIMPLE SYRUP

✦ Simple syrup is an essential ingredient in making cocktails, and it's a great idea to always keep a small bottle or jar of it in your fridge! To start, we suggest combining 1 cup (200 g) sugar with 1 cup (240 ml) water, enough for several cocktails.

✦ In a small saucepan over medium heat, combine equal parts sugar and water.

✦ Simmer, continuously stirring in circles around the edge of the pot, until the sugar is completely dissolved (approximately 2 to 3 minutes). The liquid should appear clear, not cloudy or tinted.

✦ Let cool completely, then strain into a glass bottle or jar. Seal tightly and store in the fridge for up to a month.

Shortcut

If you have a hot water dispenser or kettle, combine equal parts hot water and sugar and stir until clear.

Pink Flamingos

★ ★ ★

Our nod to the seminal and infamous John Waters film of the same name (yes, the one with the dog doodoo scene) starring Divine, this cocktail is a modification of the classic Gimlet. The Gimlet is a simple cocktail that is meant to allow the base spirit to shine through, and here the pink peppercorn perfectly represents Aries's fiery nature. Liquor infusions are an easy way to experiment with different ingredients—the possibilities are endless—and if you're unsure whether or not you want to dedicate an entire bottle of liquor to a particular infusion, you can always test it out by using only a portion of the bottle first.

GLASS TYPE

[HIGHBALL]

INGREDIENTS

2 ounces (60 ml) pink peppercorn-infused Aviation gin (instructions follow)

½ ounce (15 ml) lime juice

½ ounce (15 ml) simple syrup (instructions on previous page)

Splash of grapefruit juice

Grapefruit wedge for garnish

recipe continues

DIRECTIONS

1. Pour the pink peppercorn–infused Aviation, lime juice, simple syrup, and the grapefruit juice into a cocktail shaker.

2. Add ice and shake vigorously.

3. Strain into a highball glass filled with ice.

4. Garnish with the grapefruit wedge.

☾ MAKING PINK PEPPERCORN–INFUSED GIN

✦ Pour a bottle of gin (750 ml or 1 L) into an empty container, ideally another bottle or something with an easy-pour spout. Save the original bottle.

✦ Add 3 or 4 tablespoons pink peppercorns (1 tablespoon for each 250 ml of gin you're using). Seal container and let sit for 6 to 8 hours.

✦ Strain into the original bottle, taking care to ensure that all of the pink peppercorns are separated out.

☾ NON-ALCOHOLIC VERSION

✦ You can make this cocktail with pink peppercorn simple syrup instead of a gin infusion.

✦ To make the syrup, in a small saucepan over medium heat, combine equal parts water and sugar. Add 2 tablespoons pink peppercorns per cup (240 ml) water and simmer for 10 minutes, continuously stirring in circles around the edge of the pot to dissolve the sugar. Let steep for 6 to 8 hours before straining the syrup into a glass bottle or jar. Seal tightly and store in the fridge for up to 4 weeks.

✦ To make a nonalcoholic Pink Flamingo, combine 3 ounces (90 ml) grapefruit juice and ½ ounce (15 ml) pink peppercorn syrup and ½ ounce (15 ml) lime juice into a cocktail shaker with ice. Shake and strain into a highball glass filled with ice, then garnish with a grapefruit wedge.

Firestarter

The opening lines to the song "Firestarter" by The Prodigy describe an Aries so well: *I'm the trouble starter, punkin' instigator.* We love the extra spice that dark rum combined with cayenne adds to this recipe. A good tip is to be careful with the cayenne pepper—a small dash will do the trick. Add too much and the cocktail will become undrinkable, no matter how much you love spicy food.

GLASS TYPE

[ROCKS]

INGREDIENTS

1 ounce (30 ml) Bacardi white rum

1 ounce (30 ml) Goslings Black Seal Rum

1 ounce (30 ml) orange juice

½ ounce (15 ml) simple syrup (instructions on page 26)

Dash cayenne pepper

DIRECTIONS

1. Pour the Bacardi, Goslings, orange juice, and simple syrup into a cocktail shaker.

2. Add the dash of cayenne pepper.

3. Add ice and shake vigorously.

4. Strain into a rocks glass filled with ice.

Aries Night Life

Over the years, we've always been able to notice bold and confident Aries at the bar right away. People are attracted to your sense of adventure and ability to be honest and straightforward with people. Our nightlife tip is that people will gravitate toward you if you be yourself—but always remember to rein in your impulsivity from time to time, as it can come back to bite you.

One of our Aries customers was a magic hobbyist. He would usually come in solo and sit at the bar. He'd order a Corona with no lime and look around him. To the very first person who locked eyes with him, he'd say, "Wanna see something cool?" He would then break into a routine that generally involved spitting cards out of his mouth or making pens disappear up his nose. By that point, multiple customers at the bar would be watching, and some would gather around for a closer look. His crowd-pleasing move, which he would do when enough eyes were on him, involved pouring some of his Corona into his closed hand, then opening his hand with no liquid coming out, then showing both hands open before closing his other hand and pouring the Corona right back into the bottle. Yes, the optics of a single man in a leather jacket doing magic tricks at the bar sounds silly, but trust us: when you get a couple Margaritas in your system, you'd believe he could pull panda bears out of his ass crack.

This next story is an example of what happens when impulsiveness becomes recklessness. We were packed one night on a Saturday—the dance floor was bumping and everyone was having a great time. We heard some commotion coming from the dance floor so we walked over to check what the issue was. We saw the entire crowd from the dance floor run out to the front door in a panic. I asked one customer what happened and they responded, "The fog machine went crazy!" So we got to the empty smoky dance floor and we realized the air felt acidic and was basically unbreathable. We opened the doors to air out the dance floor and examined the fog machine. How does water-based fog juice smell like that? We reviewed the cameras and saw that at a certain point the room filled up with fog, but not from the fog machine, from another corner . . . the corner where we keep the fire extinguisher. We peeked in the corner and there was thick residue all over the ground. Yes, someone broke the fire extinguisher off the wall and blasted it into the crowd, causing everyone to stampede off the dance floor and scare the shit out of us. Luckily no one was hurt, but this was a total Aries move.

TAURUS

APRIL 20–MAY 20

You know when you're in the talking stage with your new crush and you realize your e-detective skills have failed you because you can't find any of their social media? You're down so bad that you even Google their first name plus the company they work for and "LinkedIn," but no luck there either. So you pluck up the courage to actually ask them what their Instagram is. And what could be hotter than having that person, with their cute face and cuter personality, tell you they're not on social media at all? They're just raw-dogging the world: reading books, perfecting their skincare routine, watering and playing ambient music for their plants, walking their small dog, and taking baths (for fun?!). This is what a Taurus looks like.

Taurus, for you it's natural to focus your precious time and energy only on what's truly worthy of you. You are extremely particular about your surroundings and what you'll allow into your world. You have a special love for the beautiful, the comfortable, and the soothing. If someone leaves you the keys to a dusty basement and a bucket full of nickels, you'll have that place looking like an Equinox gym bathroom, with grapefruit body wash and all, in no time. In a world where everyone is constantly fixated on chasing a train of their dreams and desires, Taurus isn't fazed and knows that the right one—whether that be a dream apartment, job, or lover—will come when the time is right.

On a Friday night, you might opt to stay in for a candlelit bubble bath, a glass of prosecco, and Kate Bush on vinyl instead of lining up for a crowded party. But okay, you might only go out and run up that hill like once a month, and that's your time to shine. If you're a Taurus, the keyword here is always going to be *stability,* but that can sometimes cross the line into stagnation. When you get in a rut, turn to a close friend to help shake you out of your routine. These songs and drinks should help.

IDEAL DATE
for a TAURUS

Your date picks you up in a drop-top baby blue 1992 Mercedes-Benz SL. You head to Whole Foods and your date says, "Get whatever you want." A few hundred dollars and a couple hours of scenic drive later, you're in a secluded oasis: just green pastures, you, your date, and the bamboo charcuterie board with assorted French fruit jams, grapes, figs, strawberries, raspberries, stuffed olives, Genoa salami, peppered salami, prosciutto, Italian dry salami, whole grain crackers with light sea salt and rosemary, brie, cheddar (aged and white), a couple crushed up lines of Lactaid (just in case), pepper jack, goat cheese, Gouda, and Havarti, and a bottle of natural wine from northern Greece with hints of pear and apple. That's it, that's the date.

♡ MODJO, "Lady (Hear Me Tonight)"

♡ SANTIGOLD, "I'm a Lady" (feat. Trouble Andrew)

♡ ARTHUR RUSSELL, "That's Us/Wild Combination"

♡ SOULWAX, "Heaven Scent" (feat. Chloe Sevigny)

♡ JULEE CRUISE, "Falling"

♡ NEON INDIAN, "Deadbeat Summer"

♡ JAY-Z & JERMAINE DUPRI, "Money Ain't a Thang"

♡ PORTISHEAD, "Glory Box"

♡ AIR, "La Femme d'Argent"

♡ DONNIE & JOE EMERSON, "Baby"

OUR TAURUS PLAYLIST

Hold Me Down

★ ★ ★

Matcha is the perfect option for Taurus, who might prefer a calmer and more uplifting substitute over coffee's erratic buzz. We love a matcha latte to switch up the daily espresso routine. Why not also try a tasty matcha cocktail for a little boost? It's caffeinated, which makes this a nice happy-hour treat. Any excess matcha that you batch can be saved for another day—it's delicious with milk, or with seltzer and a little bit of strawberry syrup.

GLASS TYPE

[ROCKS]

INGREDIENTS

1½ ounces (45 ml) Ketel One vodka

1 ounce (30 ml) matcha (instructions follow)

½ ounce (15 ml) ginger syrup (instructions follow)

¼ ounce (8 ml) lemon juice

Juniper berries for garnish

recipe continues

DIRECTIONS

1. Pour the Ketel One, matcha, ginger syrup, and lemon juice into a cocktail shaker.

2. Add ice and shake vigorously.

3. Strain into a rocks glass filled with ice.

4. Garnish with a few juniper berries.

☾ MAKING MATCHA

+ You can buy powdered matcha from any Japanese grocery store or online.

+ In a small bowl, whisk the powdered matcha with water to liquify it. We recommend following the manufacturer's instructions for suggested ratios, but to be careful you should always start with less water than you think you'll need and slowly add more to adjust.

+ We like keeping this refrigerated in a little squeeze bottle or small glass container with a speed pourer. It'll last about 3 days before it begins to lose its potency.

☾ MAKING GINGER SYRUP

+ Slice a piece of ginger (use one 1-inch/2.5-cm piece per cup/240 ml water) into thin pieces.

+ In a small saucepan over medium heat, combine equal parts sugar and water and the sliced ginger. Simmer for 10 minutes, continuously stirring in circles around the edge of the pot to dissolve the sugar. Let steep for at least 8 hours in the fridge before straining into a glass bottle or jar. Seal tightly and store in the fridge for up to 3 weeks.

☾ NONALCOHOLIC VERSION

+ Use 3 ounces (90 ml) matcha and the same ratios of all other nonalcoholic ingredients. Pour into a cocktail shaker with ice, shake, and strain into a glass with ice.

Moon Song

★ ★ ★

We love this cocktail for all our Taurus friends who have a bit of a sweet tooth. Out of all the signs, luxe and decadent Taurus is most likely to have a slice of cake for breakfast. Makgeolli is a Korean milky rice wine that tends to have a low ABV (alcohol by volume)—a stronger option for the Moon Song is to use 1 ounce (30 ml) makgeolli and 1 ounce (30 ml) of your favorite vodka. If you have difficulty finding makgeolli in person or online, you can try using a Nigori sake, which is typically unfiltered and cloudier than other types of sake. We love using fruit nectars in our cocktails, as they add a pleasingly thicker texture.

GLASS TYPE

[ROCKS]

INGREDIENTS

2 ounces (60 ml) Hana makgeolli

1½ ounces (45 ml) peach nectar

½ ounce (15 ml) lemon juice

Two blueberries for garnish

DIRECTIONS

1. Pour the Hana, peach nectar, and lemon juice into a cocktail shaker.

2. Add ice and shake vigorously.

3. Strain into a rocks glass filled with ice.

4. Garnish with two blueberries on a cocktail skewer.

Butt Massage

★ ★ ★

Taurus is the ultimate queen of chill and relaxation, and everyone deserves a nice, rejuvenating butt massage every once in a while. To that end, we made a calming CBD cocktail to soothe the nerves. This is a low-ABV cocktail featuring shochu, a Japanese rice and barley liquor, topped off with a nice fruity fizz from the Apple Sidra.

GLASS TYPE

[HIGHBALL]

INGREDIENTS

2 ounces (60 ml) Iichiko Shochu or rice wine (sake) of your choice

Apple Sidra soda or apple cider

Plant People CBD drops

Grape for garnish

DIRECTIONS

1. Pour the shochu into a highball glass filled with ice.

2. Top off with Apple Sidra.

3. Add CBD drops based on the manufacturer's instructions. We recommend starting off with less to test your tolerance.

4. Garnish with a halved grape placed on a cocktail skewer.

Pillow Talk

★ ★ ★

For our first Taurus-season special, bartender Sarah created a refreshing, herbal cocktail that typical Martini drinkers might enjoy. The Martini and all its variations are spirit-forward cocktails that are often associated with a particularly discerning and sophisticated customer, like many a Taurus. Yuzu is a tart Japanese citrus (think of a lemon having a baby with a grapefruit), and you can find small bottles of yuzu juice at any Japanese grocery store or online. A couple of drops will be enough to balance out this cocktail, but if you don't have any on hand, you can squeeze the juice out of a couple of freshly cut lemon wedges.

GLASS TYPE	INGREDIENTS
 [ROCKS]	1½ ounces (45 ml) Prairie Organic gin ½ ounce (15 ml) Dolin dry vermouth ½ ounce (15 ml) basil syrup (instructions follow) 2 drops yuzu juice Lemon wedge for garnish

DIRECTIONS

1. Pour the Prairie Organic, Dolin, basil syrup, and yuzu juice into a cocktail shaker.

2. Add ice and shake vigorously.

3. Strain into a rocks glass filled with ice.

4. Garnish with the lemon wedge.

☾ MAKING BASIL SYRUP

✦ In a small saucepan over medium heat, combine equal parts sugar and water with a large handful of basil leaves. Simmer for 10 minutes, continuously stirring in circles around the edge of the pot to dissolve the sugar. Let steep for at least 8 hours in the fridge before straining into a glass bottle or jar. Seal tightly and store refrigerated for up to 3 weeks.

Taurus Night Life

Although you aren't known to be a big partier, Taurus, you definitely like to enjoy yourself when you're out. One of the best ways to ensure you have a great night is to befriend the right people at the bar. As bar owners, we're used to people schmoozing us for potential benefits like free drinks or cutting the line outside, so that's tough to swing. The bartenders, especially on weekend nights, will be up to their necks in orders, making it difficult to get anything more than a grunt from them. So our nightlife tip to having a great time when you go out is to befriend the *bouncer*. The bouncer not only controls the flow of who gets in and who gets tossed out, they also have a direct line to the owners of the bar as well as all the bartenders. The bouncers will get you in the club, will come to your aid when some creep needs to get kicked out, and would even push through the crowd to let the bartender know that you've dropped your drink and ask for another one. Bouncers are generally large burly sequoia trees of human beings who may come off as serious, but after the monotony of checking IDs for hours, they won't mind the little bit of small talk. Bouncers have the absolute craziest stories and biggest personalities. Get to know them, always remember their name, and even if that bar or club sucks, you'll still have made a new friend.

One of our favorite bouncer stories involves a customer who tried to fight the trinity of nightlife—the owner, the bartender, and the bouncer—all in the same visit. It was a full-moon night, which means something was bound to go wrong. A young lady who was barely five-feet-one in Nike Air Max 95s asked for a drink at the crowded bar. Our bartender noticed the slur in her voice and her glassy eyes, so they handed her a glass of water instead and said "Let's just wait a little bit." She got offended and threw the water at the bartender. No matter who you are, disrespecting the bartender will get you banned, so we hurried around the bar to escort her out, and she wouldn't leave. We grabbed our bouncer, who managed to get her outside to cool off. She started yelling and called Vanessa the word that rhymes with *blunt*. (Disrespecting the owner, as it turns out, will *also* get you banned—double-banned, in this case.) She lunged toward our front door to get back inside, screaming, "I want my fucking drink!" That particular night we had two bouncers standing outside, which meant there was no way to physically get through the front door without squeezing past these two large men. But she was absolutely on a mission and started spitting at our bouncers and throwing punches. (Disrespecting the bouncer will also *definitely* get you banned.) We couldn't believe it. She continued to yell as her friend tried to get her to walk away. Next thing you know, she pulled out her cracked iPhone and screamed, "I'm calling the cops!" We stepped back inside and ten minutes later, about five or six officers rolled up, sirens blazing. We looked toward the front window and one of them was talking to this girl. We're still not sure what she was trying to achieve by calling the cops in the first place, but it didn't take long for them to figure out what was going on. Upset, she got up in this officer's face and—get this—flicked his badge. Obviously they start to handcuff her, and with her face pressed against our front windows, she screamed out, now crying with everyone watching, "I just want my fucking drink!!!"

So our Taurus nightlife tip is to be friendly to people and do exactly the opposite of this.

GEMINI

MAY 21–JUNE 20

Geminis are chaotic and charismatic, intelligent and curious; you're the life of the party. Some may say you're two-faced, but you might just as easily respond with, "What's wrong with being fake?"

A famous R&B singer and Gemini was at Mood Ring one night, and off a few rosés, she started dancing on a table with her friends cheering her on. We usually immediately escort any table dancers down because alcohol and gravity make a toxic couple, but she was famous enough that none of us were willing to confront her, so she stayed high up on that table. Very Gemini behavior. She also was very nice, complimented the staff for our good looks, and tipped generously.

On a typical Saturday evening, Gemini, you'll be found at the first of three parties you're planning on attending that night. Even though the average person can only tolerate so much small talk, you can talk for hours and hours about almost nothing, with almost anyone. You're friends with all of your exes because really, if you like someone enough to date them, why wouldn't you also like them enough to be friends? Beyond your friend count, the number of casual acquaintances you've amassed over the years is showcased in your prolific list of phone contacts. You know so many Annas you have to keep them in your phone as: Anna, Anna Kevin Friend, Anna Brunch, Anna ❄, etc. You're only ever late because you've committed to too many things. If there's a knock on you, it's that you find commitment difficult, as you're always looking for the next shiny object to chase after. In the meantime, get up on that table and show us your moves!

IDEAL DATE for a GEMINI

You and all of your exes gather in your one-bedroom apartment. The doorbell rings—it's a delivery guy and he's dropping off fifteen cases of White Claw spiked seltzer and a standard eight-slice cheese pizza. But you're a Gemini, so the line between ex and someone you used to know (and date) is thinner than your understanding of commitment, and of course there are more than eight ex-lovers in that room. Is it an orgy or are we throwing hands for the pizza? Tune in to find out.

♡ MARIYA TAKEUCHI, "Plastic Love"

♡ SYLVESTER, "You Make Me Feel (Mighty Real)"

♡ ERYKAH BADU, "Cell U Lar Device"

♡ JOJI, "Yeah Right"

♡ SAGE THE GEMINI, "Gas Pedal" (feat. Iamsu!)

♡ DOCTOR ROCKIT, "Café de Flore"
(Charles Webster's Mix)

♡ CHERRELLE, "Saturday Love"
(feat. Alexander O'Neal)

♡ BIG PUN, "Still Not a Player" (feat. Joe)

♡ MUSIQ SOULCHILD, "Just Friends (Sunny)"

PALE SAINTS, "Kinky Love"

OUR GEMINI PLAYLIST

*Dumb B**** Juice*

★ ★ ★

When we first debuted this cocktail, we were worried that some Geminis might take the name the wrong way. We were wrong: they all absolutely LOVED it! It seems that Bowen, resident Gemini, knows his people well. We Geminis enjoy getting roasted—it's called confidence, sweetie.

GLASS TYPE

[ROCKS]

INGREDIENTS

1¼ ounces (45 ml) Del Maguey Vida mezcal

½ ounce (15 ml) Ancho Reyes ancho chile liqueur

1 ounce (30 ml) mango nectar

½ ounce (15 ml) lime juice

Dash of cinnamon

Two gummy bears for garnish

DIRECTIONS

1. Pour the Del Maguey Vida, Ancho Reyes, mango nectar, and lime juice into a cocktail shaker with ice.

2. Add the dash of cinnamon and shake vigorously.

3. Strain into a rocks glass filled with ice.

4. Garnish with two gummy bears on a cocktail pick.

☾ NONALCOHOLIC VERSION

+ Rim the glass with Tajín Clásico (see pages 81). Pour 3 ounces (90 ml) mango nectar and ½ ounce (15 ml) lime juice into a cocktail shaker with ice. Add a small dash of cinnamon and shake vigorously. Strain into a rocks glass filled with ice and garnish with two gummy bears on a cocktail pick.

Uncut Geminis

★ ★ ★

Everyone enjoys a refreshing Margarita. Here, we sweeten it up with some homemade pomegranate syrup. Feel free to replace the tequila with a mezcal (we like Montelobos for this cocktail) for an extra kick. We love to describe mezcal as drinking tequila off an oak tree.

This cocktail will make you say, as a certain jeweler with big Gemini energy once did, *This is how I win.*

GLASS TYPE

[ROCKS]

INGREDIENTS

1½ ounces (45 ml) Espolòn Tequila Blanco

½ ounce (15 ml) Cointreau or triple sec

½ ounce (15 ml) pomegranate syrup (instructions follow)

½ ounce (15 ml) lime juice

Lime wheel for garnish

DIRECTIONS

1. Pour the Espolòn Tequila Blanco, Cointreau, pomegranate syrup, and lime juice into a cocktail shaker.

2. Add ice and shake vigorously.

3. Strain into a rocks glass filled with ice.

4. Garnish with a lime wheel.

☾ MAKING POMEGRANATE SYRUP

✦ In a small saucepan over medium heat, combine 3 cups each sugar (600 g) and water (720 ml). Add 3 cups (720 ml) pomegranate juice. Simmer for 10 minutes, continuously stirring in circles around the edge of the pot to dissolve the sugar. Let steep for at least 5 hours in the fridge before transferring to a glass bottle or jar. Seal tightly and store in the fridge for up to 3 weeks.

Mean Girls

★ ★ ★

Fashion wise, we love bitchy lil' purses, and drinks wise, we love sassy lil' cocktails served up in coupe glasses. This one is for all of you Geminis out there who sign your messages with "XOXO" and have eyelashes long enough to catch a half-pound of falling snow.

GLASS TYPE

[COUPE]

INGREDIENTS

1½ ounces (45 ml) Tito's vodka

1 ounce (30 ml) American Fruits Black Currant Cordial or crème de cassis

1 ounce (30 ml) cranberry juice

½ ounce (15 ml) lime juice

Strawberry slice for garnish

DIRECTIONS

1. Pour the Tito's, American Fruits, cranberry juice, and lime juice into a cocktail shaker.

2. Add ice and shake vigorously.

3. Strain into a chilled coupe glass.

4. Garnish with the strawberry slice placed on the rim of the glass.

Miss Piggy Fan Club

★ ★ ★

We take endless inspiration from the most glamorous and chic piggy (and canonical Gemini) on the planet. As an homage, we made this elegant gin and lychee-liqueur cocktail, embellished with a beautiful flower. Try one of these the next time you need an ego boost. As Miss Piggy once said, "There is no one on the planet to compare with *moi!*"

GLASS TYPE

[COUPE] OR
[NICK & NORA]

INGREDIENTS

1 ounce (30 ml) Aviation American gin

1 ounce (30 ml) Giffard Lichi-Li liqueur

1 ounce (30 ml) grapefruit juice

½ ounce (15 ml) lemon juice

Hibiscus flower or other edible flower for garnish, which can be bought at specialty grocery stores or online

DIRECTIONS

1. Pour the Aviation, Giffard Lichi-Li, grapefruit juice, and lemon juice into a cocktail shaker.

2. Add ice and shake vigorously.

3. Strain into a chilled coupe or Nick & Nora glass.

4. Garnish with the hibiscus flower.

GEMINI
Night
Life

First dates are our specialty. Bartenders and barbacks are incredibly advanced at detecting their surroundings, and we'll always take notice of anything vaguely entertaining that happens inside our space at Mood Ring.

We've seen all kinds of dates. You have the average ones with weak body language where it's obvious it isn't really going anywhere, or the couple that's been dating long enough they just sit at the bar scrolling through their phones, but just as common are the ones that result in sloppy make-out sessions (or occasionally nipple sucking) in our booths with passionate eye fucking. Once in a while, we'll get first date rock stars—people who bring first dates to Mood Ring two, three, four times a week. Service people in nightlife are sworn to unspoken secrecy: if you're a serial dater and you come in with a new date, we just act like we've never seen you before in our entire lives. Some of these serial "daters" have a system down, a recipe—except you replace the salt with a navy cardigan, the pepper with the comfy corner booth with the most flattering lighting, and butter with the same recycled (but proven) jokes.

happy together

There's a more special flavor of first dates, too. We had two regulars, a couple, who would come in two, or maybe more, times per week, always at around 8 P.M. They always sat in the same booth, asked for the same drink orders, were kind and tipped well, and lo and behold, a few minutes later a third person, different each time, would join them. The third would say hello in the way you greet people you meet for the first time. We're willing to bet it all that at least one half of that couple was a Gemini, maybe both. (Actually, if you're the couple reading this right now, please reach out—we need to know.)

So do the math here: if you're having a threesome with a new person at least twice a week for a year, after a year-plus you might just dry up the well of the Brooklyn unicorn scene. And one day the couple mentions that they're moving to Los Angeles. One of us by chance ends up in an LA bar a few months later, and behind the bar the cocktailian (hah) is none other than one-half of this couple. A new city, a new stable of unicorns, a new world.

So for all the no-rules Geminis constantly seeking adventure or chaos in their lives, when you've found something you enjoy, whether it's crocheting arm sweaters or engaging in hot New York City air-conditioned threesomes, our tip is to focus on that thing you enjoy and figure out how to do it again and again, really experiencing all it has to offer before you move on to the next shiny thing.

CANCER

JUNE 21–JULY 22

ancer, this chapter is an ode to all the times you've ugly-cried at the seafood restaurant, tears seasoning your rock shrimp and mussels, as strangers looked on while pretending not to. Or, if you have a flair for the dramatic, the times you've just jogged around the track for hours and hours until you sweated enough that there were no more tears left to cry. The password to all your accounts might be "Love you for ten thousand years," as Takeshi Kaneshiro said in *Chungking Express*. You can't help but internalize all the emotions of those close to you while throwing your own feelings on top of that pile the same way we all put clothes and then more clothes on that one chair in our bedroom.

Even if you're not a Cancer, you've had your Cancer moments, and these recipes are a special thank-you to all the brave people wearing their hearts on their sleeves.

If vulnerability were a town, Cancer would be the mayor, and that's a good thing! You're in tune with your emotions and those of the people closest to you, which makes you a great friend and emotional companion. You're a true romantic to the end, and just reading the words "you wanna cuddle?" has you thinking about the person you'd love to cuddle right now. We won't judge you if it's your ex. You love stability and consistency, but you should remember that sometimes it's okay to break from your own traditions and nostalgic obsessions—your sad-songs-to-cry-to playlist will still be on queue when you get home.

IDEAL DATE
for a CANCER

It's 70.5 degrees Fahrenheit, 35 percent humidity, there's a 10–15 mile per hour fresh breeze, and it's sunny, but only SPF-30 sunny, with clouds that look like they're trying to tell you something important. You and your date drive to a therapeutic petting zoo of nonthreatening animals. We're talking bunnies, miniature horses, alpacas, guinea pigs, Patagonian maras, and of course the baby wallabies. How could we forget the baby wallabies? You're so overwhelmed by the cuteness you start crying, and you hold hands with your date and call each other special while maintaining eye contact. You're special. No, you're special. Tears.

♡ MAZZY STAR, "Fade into You"

♡ KELSEY LU, "Shades of Blue"

♡ TANUKICHAN, "Lazy Love"

♡ THE CURE, "In Between Days"

♡ FRANK OCEAN, "Dear April"

♡ CRAYON, "Give You Up" (Darius Remix)
(feat. KLP)

♡ DIRTY BEACHES, "Lord Knows Best"

♡ AMADOU & MARIAM, "Sabali"

♡ COCTEAU TWINS, "Heaven or Las Vegas"

♡ SNEAKER PIMPS, "Six Underground"

OUR CANCER PLAYLIST

Be My Teddy Bear

★ ★ ★

This cocktail is the liquid version of a weighted blanket with a soft body pillow, the faint glow of the humidifier in the corner of your warm bedroom while snow gently falls outside the window. Isn't that nice? We love this bourbon cocktail because of its aromatic depth and hint of sour from the tart cherry juice, and we recommend that people who don't usually gravitate toward whisky cocktails give this one a chance.

GLASS TYPE

[ROCKS]

INGREDIENTS

1½ ounces (45 ml) Maker's Mark bourbon

1 ounce (30 ml) Midori Japanese melon liqueur

½ ounce (15 ml) tart cherry juice

½ ounce (15 ml) lemon juice

Amarena cherry for garnish

DIRECTIONS

1. Pour the Maker's Mark, Midori, cherry juice, and lemon juice into a cocktail shaker.

2. Add ice and shake vigorously.

3. Strain into a rocks glass filled with ice.

4. Garnish with an Amarena cherry.

Fade Into You

★ ★ ★

We named this cocktail after the iconic Mazzy Star song. What's more emotional than Hope Sandoval crooning "I want to hold the hand inside you," a feeling every Cancer knows all too well? We love playing with the Combier line of liqueurs from France, and for this cocktail we chose their Pamplemousse (grapefruit flavor). Suze, which is a Swiss aperitif, adds nice floral and citrus notes to this cocktail.

GLASS TYPE

[HIGHBALL]

INGREDIENTS

2 ounces (60 ml) Prairie Organic gin

¾ ounce (23 ml) Combier Crème de Pamplemousse Rose or other grapefruit liqueur

½ ounce (15 ml) Suze or other bitter aperitif

½ ounce (15 ml) lime juice

Seltzer

Thyme sprig for garnish

DIRECTIONS

1. Pour the Prairie Organic, Combier, Suze, and lime juice into a cocktail shaker.

2. Add ice and shake vigorously.

3. Strain into a highball glass filled with ice.

4. Top with a splash of seltzer.

5. Garnish with a thyme sprig.

I'm Not Crying, You Are

★ ★ ★

We are huge fans of Amaro Nonino, which is delicious served neat or on the rocks. Amari are Italian liqueurs that are generally known for being bitter (*amaro* means "bitter" in Italian), but they can also be sweeter depending on the particular one you're drinking. If you once tried Fernet—which is just Jägermeister wearing a Rolex, let's be real—and were put off by the strong menthol taste, don't just write off all Amari. This recipe is a nice place to start. We love Mountain Valley seltzer because the bubbles hold for days, so a bottle sits great in your refrigerator if you need a few days to finish. This cocktail has layers of flavor, with the combination of the earthy Amaro, the sweet citrus of orange, and the herbal rosemary—similar to the onion-like personalities of a Cancer (they're layered and also make you want to cry).

GLASS TYPE	INGREDIENTS
 [ROCKS]	1¾ ounces (53 ml) Amaro Nonino or other sweet Amaro ½ ounce (15 ml) Dolin sweet vermouth 1½ ounces (45 ml) orange juice Mountain Valley seltzer, or other seltzer of your choice Rosemary twig for garnish

recipe continues

DIRECTIONS

1. Pour the Amaro Nonino, Dolin, and orange juice into a cocktail shaker.
2. Add ice and shake vigorously.
3. Strain into a rocks glass filled with ice.
4. Top with a splash of seltzer.
5. Garnish with a rosemary twig.

Our Favorite Amari

AMARO NONINO

If we didn't make it obvious enough, this is our amaro of choice. A bit on the sweeter side, any time a customer offers to buy us a shot you'll likely see us reaching for this bottle on our top shelf.

CYNAR

Pronounced CHEE-nar, this is an extremely versatile amaro. Try using it as a substitute for other bitter liqueurs, like Campari in the classic Negroni (make it with ¾ ounce your gin of choice, ¾ ounce Cynar, and ¾ ounce sweet vermouth, stirred and garnished with an orange peel).

AMARO MONTENEGRO

Last but not least, we love making a simple nightcap consisting of 1 oz Amaro Montenegro and 1 oz mezcal, stirred. Simple, quick, and gets the job done.

𝕶iss 𝕸e, 𝕴'm 𝕰mo

★ ★ ★

If it seems tedious to go to a supermarket, slap some watermelons to check for ripeness, and take one home to blend, please hear us out. Wait until a hot summer day and bust out some cold watermelon if you like enjoying your life. Here, we've also added a cucumber infusion that takes two days to steep and just the right amount of bubbles from a splash of ginger beer to create a refreshing and seriously satisfying cocktail. We wanted to make a cocktail that featured one of the wateriest fruits for our teary-eyed Cancers. I'm not okay, I promise.

GLASS TYPE

[ROCKS]

INGREDIENTS

1½ ounces (45 ml) cucumber-infused Tito's vodka (instructions follow)

½ ounce (15 ml) St. Germain elderflower liqueur

1¼ ounce (8 ml) fresh watermelon juice (instructions follow)

½ ounce (15 ml) lime juice

Ginger beer

Dill frond for garnish

recipe continues

DIRECTIONS

1. Pour the cucumber-infused Tito's, St. Germain, watermelon juice, and lime juice into a cocktail shaker.

2. Add ice and shake vigorously.

3. Strain into a rocks glass filled with ice.

4. Top with a splash of ginger beer.

5. Garnish with a dill frond.

☾ MAKING CUCUMBER-INFUSED VODKA

✦ Pour a bottle of Tito's vodka (750 ml or 1 L) into an empty container, ideally another bottle or something with an easy-pour spout. Save the original bottle.

✦ Cut one cucumber into thin slices, add to the container, and seal.

✦ Let sit in a cool, dry place for 2 days. (If you're trying to impress the friends tonight, put the sliced cucumber in a container with the vodka and shake as hard as you can for as long as you can—you'll manage to get some of the cucumber into the vodka this way.)

✦ Strain into the original bottle, taking care to ensure that all of the cucumbers are separated out.

☾ MAKING FRESH WATERMELON JUICE

✦ Cut a seedless watermelon into chunks small enough to fit inside your blender.

✦ Blend until liquefied.

✦ Strain into a glass bottle or jar. Watermelon juice will keep for 2 to 3 days in the fridge.

☾ NONALCOHOLIC VERSION

✦ In a cocktail shaker, muddle 3 thin slices of cucumber. Add 3 ounces (90 ml) watermelon juice and ½ ounce (15 ml) lime juice. Add ice, then shake and strain into a rocks glass filled with ice. Top off with ginger beer and garnish with a dill frond.

cancer

Night

Life

As we said earlier in this chapter, crying in public is more than okay. If it makes you feel better, none of us behind the bar are judging or making fun of you. Mostly we want to make sure you're okay while not getting in your personal business. Our role, outside of providing drinks and enjoyable banter, is to make sure you feel safe and welcome in our space.

Once in a while, we have to check in on the bathrooms if someone has been in one of the stalls for too long. Usually it's someone who ate a check their ass can't cash (bad burrata for dinner) or drank a little too much and they are vomiting. But one weekend night, the bar was packed, the horny juices were in the air thick as fog, and one of our customers notified us that someone had been in the bathroom for a little too long.

We grabbed our flashlights and wove through the crowd toward the bathrooms. By this point the line was filled with desperate bladders and matching facial expressions. We knocked on the door, no response. We knocked again, no response. Now we were worried. Situations like these call for us to take out the master bathroom key. We knocked one more time, and after no response we opened up the stall door with nosy customers trying to peek over our shoulders. We were half expecting a drunk, passed-out customer on the ground, but instead we saw a young lady bawling her eyes out on the toilet on the phone. Mind you, there was blaring techno music coming from the dancefloor, but in between drums, we heard the words: *"I fucking love you!!!"* She noticed us at the door, got up, and apologized. We don't like people walking out by themselves in a bad mental state, so we escorted her outside to a bench and brought her water. She started talking about how her girlfriend broke up with her on their anniversary and how she thought they would spend the rest of their lives together and now everything is shit. Now we felt bad for her. We asked her how long they were dating. With tears flowing freely from her eyes, she said, "Tonight was our two-week anniversary."

    While *Crying in the Club on the Toilet* would be a great name for an album, if you're feeling that two-week relationship breakup vulnerability, we recommend surrounding yourself with the people and things that make you feel good rather than locking yourself away in a bar bathroom with your phone. Thank us later.

LEO

JULY 23–AUGUST 22

oted most likely to celebrate their birthdays two times a year (petition to normalize quarter birthdays incoming), Leos are the divas of the zodiac. We can learn a lot from you Leos: confidence, pizzazz, and a sense of loyalty all come naturally to you. Your symbol is the proud lion, and you have a larger-than-life personality (and possibly a bedazzled trucker hat) to match. You aren't one to shy away from the spotlight, so whether you're more Mufasa (angel) or Scar (devil), you might be the one to demand access to the aux plug in the Uber ride home because the driver absolutely needs to hear you belt out Lady Gaga at 4:05 A.M. Five-star ratings all around!

Leos can't get enough of praise and adoration, but you are equally generous and giving toward your closest friends and loved ones. You see so much beauty and romance in the world, and all you want is someone to share it with. If someone is lucky enough to date you, they should always remember to express their gratitude and never make the dangerous mistake of taking their precious Leo for granted, because once you feel scorned, there's no going back. Your pride is the chair that supports your dump-truck personality but also the legs that prop up your (sometimes inflated) ego. Leos make great reality TV contestants because drama is just the shadow that follows you everywhere you go, and yes, you look great from every angle.

IDEAL DATE
for a LEO

You invite your date to a kitschy bar: red sequin walls, purple streamers you find on your clothes for months, that sexy, stockinged leg lamp from *A Christmas Story*, and a Moscow Mule strong enough to remind you that you have Pedialyte in the fridge at home. As you and your date sit down, your date notices there's a stage and large sign that reads: OPEN MIC SIGN-UPS. You say to your date, "I mean, fine, if you're gonna pressure me, I'll do one song." You sign up, and a few minutes later, you're belting out Adele's "Someone Like You" to a crowd that recognizes your vocal range, your passion, your dedication to the craft, and those shoes—*wow, what a look*—as they whisper among themselves and pull out their phones because this is good enough to go viral. On the way back to your seat after the song, you put in your earplugs because the clapping is deafening. Everyone tells you they love you and you're so talented. *Who, me? Oh, no, oh, come on.* Your date has fallen in love in 4 minutes 45 seconds.

♡ FLOORPLAN, "Tell You No Lie"

♡ MARIAH CAREY, "Shake It Off"

♡ GRACE JONES, "La Vie en Rose"

♡ SISTER SLEDGE, "Lost in Music"

♡ CAM'RON, "Hey Ma" (feat. Juelz Santana)

♡ SINÉAD O'CONNOR, "Nothing Compares 2 U"

♡ PEACHES, "Set It Off"

♡ LOOSE JOINTS, "Is It All Over My Face?"
(Masters at Work Remix)

♡ SAVAGE GARDEN, "Truly Madly Deeply"

♡ EVE, "Let Me Blow Ya Mind" (feat. Gwen Stefani)

OUR LEO PLAYLIST

Me, Myself & I

★ ★ ★

When our bartender Randall introduced the Me, Myself & I, it was a revelation: we loved the flavor profile from the strawberry sage shrub. If you're unsure about putting vinegar in your drink, don't worry—its acidity is balanced out by fresh strawberries here. We also love the fragrant balance afforded by the floral aperitif Lillet Blanc. The flamboyant pink and magenta color of this cocktail, as well as the bold flavors of the shrub and mezcal, match the extravagant personalities of the Broadway-headlining Leo.

GLASS TYPE

[ROCKS]

INGREDIENTS

1½ ounces (45 ml) Banhez Mezcal Joven

½ ounce (15 ml) Lillet Blanc or other fruity aperitif

¾ ounces (12 ml) strawberry sage shrub (instructions follow)

½ ounce (15 ml) lemon juice

Sage leaf for garnish

recipe continues

DIRECTIONS

1. Pour the Banhez Mezcal Joven, Lillet Blanc, strawberry sage shrub, and lemon juice into a cocktail shaker.

2. Add ice and shake vigorously.

3. Strain into a rocks glass filled with ice.

4. Garnish with the sage leaf.

☾ MAKING THE STRAWBERRY SAGE SHRUB

✦ First, make strawberry sage simple syrup: In a small saucepan over medium heat, combine equal parts sugar and water. Add approximately 4 hulled strawberries per cup (240 ml) water. Simmer for 10 minutes, continuously stirring in circles around the edge of the pot to dissolve the sugar. Remove from the heat and stir in 15 sage leaves. Let cool completely, then strain into a glass bottle or jar. Seal tightly and store in the fridge for up to 3 weeks.

✦ Combine 2 cups (480 ml) strawberry sage syrup, 1½ cups (360 ml) apple cider vinegar, and ½ cup (120 ml) water to make the strawberry sage shrub. Transfer to another glass bottle or jar, seal tightly, and store in the fridge for up to 6 months.

Best You Ever Had

★ ★ ★

This cocktail is a fun way to use any leftover strawberry sage syrup you might have from making the Me, Myself & I. Passion fruit is one of our favorite juices to play with because its slightly tart sweetness adds a nice tropical flavor to any cocktail. If you can find passion-fruit nectar, we love the additional texture it adds to every cocktail. Passion fruit is a unique and sensual fruit, and—we're looking you right in the eyes, you Leos—you are a unique and sensual fruit as well.

GLASS TYPE

[ROCKS]

INGREDIENTS

2 ounces (60 ml) Hornitos Plata tequila

2 ounces (60 ml) passion-fruit juice

½ ounce (15 ml) lime juice

¼ ounce (8 ml) Strawberry Sage Syrup (opposite page)

Thyme sprig for garnish

DIRECTIONS

1. Pour the Hornitos Plata, passion-fruit juice, lime juice, and strawberry syrup into a cocktail shaker.

2. Add ice and shake vigorously.

3. Strain into a rocks glass filled with ice.

4. Garnish with the thyme sprig.

Catwalk Cutie

★ ★ ★

This is a quick and refreshing cocktail that you can whip up at your next party or throw in your ex's face if you're feeling toxic that day. Leo is a summertime sign, so for this season we love to play with fruity flavors that are bold and perfect for a hot summer day. Calamansi is a citrus (looks like a round lime, tastes like something between a lemon and an orange) from the Philippines that you can find at any Filipino grocery store or online. Tajín Clásico is one of our favorite cocktail seasonings, and we find that the extra spice complements tequila much better than plain ol' salt. If you have any leftovers, throw it on some mango for a nice snack.

GLASS TYPE

[HIGHBALL]

INGREDIENTS

Tajín Clásico seasoning

2 ounces (60 ml) Espolòn Blanco tequila

1 ounce (30 ml) calamansi juice, or fresh lime juice

Lime wedge for garnish

DIRECTIONS

1. Rim a highball glass with Tajín then fill the glass with ice.
2. Pour the Espolòn Blanco and calamansi juice into a cocktail shaker.
3. Add ice and shake vigorously.
4. Strain into the highball glass.
5. Garnish with the lime wedge.

NOTE

Rims are used in cocktails to add a kick of flavor and complement or contrast particular flavors—think of the classic tart and citrusy Margarita with its salt rim. We use a special glass rimmer at the bar, but for the home bartender we recommend rubbing a lime wedge around the rim of your empty glass and dipping it onto a plate full of the salt or seasoning to coat.

☾ NONALCOHOLIC VERSION:

✦ Rim a highball glass with Tajín, then add ice.

✦ Pour 3 ounces (90 ml) calamansi juice and ½ ounce (15 ml) simple syrup (instructions on page 26) into a cocktail shaker. Add ice, shake, and strain into the glass. Top off with seltzer. Garnish with a lime wedge.

World's Tiniest Violin

You can't help but feel like Swarovski crystals on a hotel rooftop bar when sipping on this frothy lavender-tinted cocktail. We love the texture from the egg white as it soothes the gentle bite of the vodka. You're allowed to be mean to people when you're sipping on this one (not that you needed any encouragement on that front, Leos).

GLASS TYPE

[COUPE]

INGREDIENTS

2 ounces (60 ml) Reyka vodka

½ ounce (15 ml) Combier Liqueur de Violette or other crème de violette

½ ounce (15 ml) lemon juice

2 drops of Angostura bitters

1 egg white

Dried lavender for garnish

DIRECTIONS

1. Pour the Reyka, Combier, and lemon juice into a cocktail shaker.

2. Add two drops of angostura bitters and the egg white.

3. First, do a dry shake (do not add any ice).

4. Add ice and shake again, vigorously.

5. Strain into a chilled coupe glass.

6. Garnish with dried lavender.

Raw Egg Warning

Consuming raw or lightly cooked eggs poses a risk of food-borne illness.

LEO

Night Life

As a proud Leo, you love to be the center of attention at a bar, whether it's acquaintances admiring your incredible sense of style (four-inch heels revealing an ankle monitor on a Tuesday??) or strangers hanging on to your every word (can't spell personality without the letters L-E-O). Well, our nightlife tip for you concerns the age-old question: What is a proper tip? In most American service industry jobs, the hourly rate is generally on the lower side, so the bulk of your bartender's income comes from tips. A standard tip is 20 percent, and if paying with cash, $1 per drink is also pretty standard. If you have the means and enjoyed the service, feel free to tip more.

But why are we telling you this? If you're a Leo, you love to go all out, and you sure as hell make sure that people see it. When a loud and proud Leo storms the bar, we notice these personalities right away. Sometimes we make a note to keep an eye on this person to make sure they're not starting trouble; other times we just enjoy watching this energetic human tornado stomping around.

On one busy night, a gentleman came in wearing what we can only describe as the kind of outfit a detective might wear on a night out while undercover but clearly not undercover enough. He was wearing a loose plaid shirt slightly unbuttoned, with a trucker hat and jeans. This wasn't our usual clientele, so we noticed him right away. He walked up to the bar and ordered two shots of Patrón, which is usually a show-off order. We brought the shots, and when it was time to pay, he hesitated and looked around. We noticed his friend next to him, seemingly annoyed. Then the detective yelled, "Count the number of people in here and I'll tip you $5 for every person in this bar right now!" His friend let out a big sigh and said, "Dude, you can't do this at every fucking bar we go to." A few customers were looking over at this point. Making your bartender or server jump through hoops for a tip is very odd behavior, but when he pulled out a roll of cash in a rubber band, you bet your ass we did a head count. The man's friend came up later in the night to apologize and said that the big tipper had just gotten out of prison and didn't know how to act.

We love a Leo who shows up with a wholesome bang.

VIRGO

AUGUST 23–SEPTEMBER 22

You know when you and your besties plan a little getaway and there's that one friend who has the itinerary printed out and books the Airbnb because they have the best rating and brings extra Costco-brand toothbrushes and socks for everyone? Yes, the rare breed of person with only one alarm in the morning because they get up without needing to hit snooze? I'm talking about you, you brainy Virgos.

Virgos, you make great friends with Air signs (Gemini, Aquarius, Libra) because you counterbalance the chaos of their Air sign with your desire to "fix" people, like in that one Coldplay song. You also love the carefree attitudes of these Air signs, as you're able to live vicariously through them while staying fixated on achieving perfection (even though subconsciously you know that no one is perfect). But you may also gravitate toward a more grounded sign like Taurus, someone who will be able to reciprocate the appreciation and thoughtfulness you often provide for others.

Virgos make caring and generous lovers, and our only recommendation is to get out of your own head once in a while and push away those insecurities. You probably don't need to worry about whether or not your partner of three years who moved across the country to be with you, gives you foot rubs, and bakes you vegan mac and cheese every night actually loves you. Just enjoy it and focus on getting your own needs met once in a while.

IDEAL DATE
for a VIRGO

You meet at Target in the suburbs and spend two hours picking out every cleaning supply, organizational essential, and piece of storage furniture known to your part of the world. You go to your date's apartment and spit on the ground in disgust: there's a bath towel on the door, three unfinished bottles of water on the coffee table, dust bunnies the size of baby racoons, and let's not even get started on the hair in the *kitchen* sink. You and your date spend the afternoon in perfect harmony cleaning and organizing the apartment. It's a good thing your date absolutely maxed out on the acts of service portion of the Love Language test. When the place is all lemon-scented and sparkling, cables hidden, and remote controls organized by length order, you sit down and appreciate the good work. You then make love, eyes closed, missionary style, on the memory foam mattress. (That last part is a joke—we know you studied all the available positions on the internet.)

♡ THE HUMAN LEAGUE, "Seconds"

♡ SZA, "Good Days"

♡ YASUAKI SHIMIZU, "Umi No Ue Kara"

♡ YO LA TENGO, "You Can Have It All"

♡ THE CRANBERRIES, "Analyse"

♡ SLEIGH BELLS, "Rill Rill"

♡ MIKE HUCKABY, "The Jazz Republic"

♡ DARONDO, "Didn't I"

♡ THE KNIFE, "Pass This On"

♡ BAHAMADIA, "Uknowhowwedu"

OUR VIRGO PLAYLIST

Suffering from Success

★ ★ ★

This drink was once devised to vaguely taste like cleaning fluid (only natural for fussy, anal-retentive Virgo). It's actually really good, but if it's your first time drinking Cynar (an amaro featuring artichoke), you may have to adjust to its bitter flavor. That said, this is one of our all-time most popular cocktails, created by of one of our bartenders, Sarah Rosenblatt. In true Virgo fashion, she began planning the recipe about six months ahead of time. Virgos, we hope you never change.

GLASS TYPE

[ROCKS]

INGREDIENTS

1 ounce (30 ml) Tito's vodka

1 ounce (30 ml) Cynar or Amaro of your choice

¾ ounces (23 ml) lemongrass syrup (instructions follow)

½ ounce (15 ml) lemon juice

Ginger peeled into ribbons for garnish

DIRECTIONS

1. Pour the Tito's, Cynar, lemongrass syrup, and lemon juice into a cocktail shaker.

2. Add ice and shake vigorously.

3. Strain into a rocks glass filled with ice.

4. Garnish with a ginger ribbon.

☾ MAKING LEMONGRASS SYRUP

✦ In a small saucepan over medium heat, combine equal parts sugar and water. Add sliced lemongrass stalks (two stalks per cup/240 ml water) to the pot. Simmer for 10 minutes, continuously stirring in circles around the edge of the pot to dissolve the sugar. Let cool completely, then strain into a glass bottle or jar. Seal tightly and store in the fridge for up to 3 weeks.

Marie Kondo

★ ★ ★

We love this organizational queen (surprisingly, not a Virgo) for her apparent sweetness but also her ability to deliver some harsh truths. So here we play with the balance between ingredients that are light and fruity and those that are deeper and spicier. As a note, the black peppercorn syrup will last for at least three weeks in your fridge, so make extra and play around with it to lend some added depth to your cocktails.

GLASS TYPE	INGREDIENTS
[COUPE]	1½ ounces (45 ml) Tito's vodka
	1½ ounces (45 ml) grapefruit juice
	½ ounce (15 ml) black peppercorn syrup (instructions follow)
	2 dashes Fee Brothers cardamom bitters
	Rosemary sprig for garnish

DIRECTIONS

1. Pour the Tito's, grapefruit juice, and black peppercorn syrup into a cocktail shaker with ice.

2. Add two dashes of cardamom bitters and shake vigorously.

3. Strain into a chilled coupe glass.

4. Garnish with a rosemary sprig.

☾ MAKING THE BLACK PEPPERCORN SYRUP:

✦ In a small saucepan over medium heat, combine equal parts sugar and water. Simmer for 10 minutes, continuously stirring in circles around the edge of the pot to dissolve the sugar. Remove from the heat, add ¼ cup (24 g) black peppercorns per cup (240 ml) water, and let steep for 20 minutes. Strain into a glass bottle or jar. Seal tightly and store in the fridge for up to 3 weeks.

I Like You a Latte

★ ★ ★

If you're looking for an Adderall in cocktail form, look no further. You will need an espresso maker (or substitute your strongest coffee) and a milk frother, which can be bought for around $20–$30. This cocktail can be served either iced or hot.

If you'd like to make this more of a dessert-time treat, the oat milk can be replaced with two scoops of vanilla ice cream, and the Kahlúa and espresso can be poured over the scoops for an alcoholic affogato.

GLASS TYPE

[ROCKS]

INGREDIENTS

2 ounces (60 ml) Kahlúa coffee liqueur

½ ounce (15 ml) demerara syrup (instructions follow)

Espresso shot

4 ounces (120 ml) frothed oat milk

Espresso beans for garnish

DIRECTIONS

1. Pour the Kahlúa, demerara syrup, and espresso shot into a rocks glass; use a bar spoon to stir.

2. Add ice (optional).

3. Add the frothed milk to the glass.

4. Garnish with a few espresso beans.

🌙 MAKING DEMERARA SYRUP:

✦ In a small saucepan over medium heat, combine equal parts demerara sugar (or brown sugar cubes) and water. Simmer for 10 minutes.

The Devil's in the Prada

This cocktail is designed to help Virgo loosen up a bit, because no matter how clean cut and perfectly polished someone may be, it's important to roll around in the mud every once in a while. Mezcal paired with orange is just one of those underrated combos that never misses. And it's not every day that you see Worcestershire sauce in a cocktail, but the hint of tang it brings, along with the sweet citrus of the orange and the smoky mezcal, makes this an easy cocktail to down. Brace yourself for the nice little sting as it hits your throat!

GLASS TYPE

[ROCKS]

INGREDIENTS

2 ounces (60 ml) Montelobos Espadín mezcal

½ ounce (15 ml) lime juice

A few dashes Worcestershire sauce (if you're vegetarian or vegan, you can look for a vegan Worcestershire sauce brand like Annie's)

Tajín Clásico seasoning

Orange slice for garnish

DIRECTIONS

1. Pour the Montelobos Espadín, lime juice, and Worcestershire sauce into a cocktail shaker.

2. Add ice and shake vigorously.

3. Strain into a rocks glass filled with ice.

4. For garnish, generously sprinkle Tajín onto the orange slice. Add it to the rim. Have fun sucking on it as you gradually finish your cocktail.

☾ NONALCOHOLIC VERSION

✦ Substitute the mezcal with your favorite seltzer and skip the Worcestershire sauce. Our favorite seltzer is from Mountain Valley Spring Water. Squeeze juice from 2 to 3 lime wedges, add 2 drops of orange bitters, and garnish with a Tajín-sprinkled orange slice.

Virgo Night Life

There can be so many stressful moments in a crowded bar, especially for a Virgo. The loud music, the rowdy customers, the wait for the bathroom line or when trying to order at the bar. The anxiety that comes with maneuvering through all the other thirsty customers to get the bartender's attention can remind you of your last punk show when someone yelled, "Let's mosh!" and next thing you knew, your glasses and left shoe were missing. We know the exact feeling of getting up to order another drink, seeing the sea of people all yelling at the bartenders, and just giving up and sitting back down defeated.

Here are some helpful tips for ordering at the bar to minimize the chaos and stress without having anyone yell at you. Now, unless you're six-foot-eight or literally Rihanna, you'll have to get the bartender's attention the old-fashioned way: direct but not abrasive. Human beings can sense when other people are looking at them, and while bartending, we feel many eyeballs on us, but if you're standing right at the bar and not looking at us we probably think you don't need anything. If you're looking at a bartender and they lock eyes with you, you're immediately on their radar. Even if they have a million things to do before getting to you, you are on their mental checklist. Once you lock eyes, you can wait for them to come to you, or even saying a quick "Hi!" is totally fine. If you're positioned like you need something, wallet or card in hand, and have your order ready, it makes the transaction much smoother, and when you need to come back and reorder your bartender will remember that and prioritize you. We love it when our customers make things easy for us.

When you're at a packed bar or club, it's helpful to be ready for a few potential questions from your bartender:

1. What can I get for you?
2. How many?
3. Rocks or neat?
4. Cash or card?
5. Open or close?

The fifth question is the one many people get tripped up on—it's just asking if you'd like to start a tab and keep the card on file or close out and pay for all the drinks right now.

Some absolute no-nos we've encountered before are:

1. Please don't touch us (i.e., a tap on our hand to get our attention) or snap your fingers—so rude
2. It's not helpful to yell your order when we haven't acknowledged we're ready to take your order (the word TECATE echoes in our ears to this day).
3. If you seem intoxicated (swaying around, eyes glazed) don't even try to order until you're a bit more composed.

There was one time when an actor from a popular Netflix series (think Katy Perry in prison) was at the bar and looking to order. He yelled out his order, and when we didn't acknowledge him, he said, "Do you know who I am?" One of us looked closely at his face and responded with, "Absolutely not." One of our customers let us know afterward who he was. The show is great, by the way. But while we know we might look like robots behind the bar slinging drink after drink, you have to remember that we service workers are all in fact human beings. Do you kiss your mother with that mouth?

There you have it: our Virgo nightlife tip. Be respectful and you will get that respect back. And don't stress, my beautiful Virgos, there are worse things than not getting a drink at a bar . . .

LIBRA

SEPTEMBER 23–OCTOBER 22

ave you ever met someone who falls in love exactly 5.5 times per year and thought to yourself: "That looks not very fun at all"? Let's just say the Libra has a doctorate in mingling and another in romance. Though often drunk in love, Libras are very picky and particular about their life partners. And when it comes to friendship, Libra, you're a social butterfly who makes sure to catch up with every last person in the room—you hate for anyone to feel left out. You have a great sense of fairness that comes in handy when it becomes necessary to mediate all kinds of tiffs between your friends. People trust you because they know your intentions are good and your opinions are balanced, but your ability to tunnel-vision on the logical rather than the emotional (only when it comes to other people's problems, of course) can be frustrating to them at times.

We have to remember Libras are Air signs! Libras are the type to eat avocado toast with sesame seeds for breakfast every single day and then all of a sudden they've moved on to a blackberry açaí bowl every morning without looking back—rinse and repeat. This means you Libras can be hard to predict at times and therefore potentially unreliable. Confrontation causes you anxiety, and you try to avoid it at all costs, but try to remember that sometimes it's a necessary part of resolving issues with friends or lovers. Find the people who will stimulate and challenge you and hold on to those precious souls. They'll be lucky to have you.

IDEAL DATE
for a LIBRA

People need to realize that when they date you, Libra, they're dating the whole team. You're a package deal. As in, you're a sexy Big Mac but don't forget the fries. If your friends don't like your lover, you'll be in a tight spot choosing between your lover and your friends. Just kidding—you'll side with your friends every time. So you pick your favorite tapas restaurant as a way to gauge if you're compatible with your date. And what do you know, your friends happen to also be eating at the restaurant. Is this slight manipulation—did you plan this—or is it just coincidence? That's between you and the group chat. You ask your date if they mind if your friends join. They don't mind. So yes, your ideal date is really all of your friends hanging out together with a stranger from Hinge. On the jukebox in the background, War's "Why Can't We Be Friends?" starts playing. You think to yourself, *Truly, why can't we all be friends (or lovers)?*

♡ MOTHER FUNK, "Sunshine"

♡ HERCULES & LOVE AFFAIR, "Blind"
(Frankie Knuckles Remix)

♡ KINDNESS, "Gee Up"

♡ JAPANESE BREAKFAST, "Diving Woman"

♡ CAKES DA KILLA, "Luv Me Nots"

♡ SOPHIE ELLIS-BEXTOR,
"Murder on the Dancefloor"

♡ THE BRIAN JONESTOWN MASSACRE, "Anemone"

♡ SUMMER WALKER, "Come Thru" (feat. Usher)

♡ TÉLÉPOPMUSIK, "Breathe"

♡ THE BEE GEES, "Love You Inside Out"

OUR LIBRA PLAYLIST

PLUR

★ ★ ★

PLUR is Peace, Love, Unity, Respect. It's exchanging candy bracelets at the rave, and back before we knew better, drinking water from strangers' backpacks. Libras have PLUR tattooed all over their foreheads.

We absolutely love using St. Germain elderflower; it spruces up any recipe with a sweet floral flavor. It's especially delicious when topped off with bubbly prosecco. With gin, we like using Aviation brand because of its botanical selections during distilling (coriander, juniper, lavender)—and feel free to try out Aviation Old Tom gin specifically, which is barrel-aged in whiskey barrels and makes for a smoother overall flavor.

GLASS TYPE

[WINE GLASS]

INGREDIENTS

1½ ounces (45 ml) Aviation gin

½ ounce (15 ml) St. Germain elderflower liqueur

Prosecco

Mint sprig for garnish

recipe continues

DIRECTIONS

1. Pour the Aviation and St. Germain into a mixing glass.

2. Add ice to fill the mixing glass about halfway and use a bar spoon to stir.

3. Strain into a wine glass filled with ice.

4. Top with prosecco.

5. Garnish with a mint sprig.

Note

This spritz cocktail is also easy to make variations of. Feel free to swap out the elderflower liqueur with other options. Here are some fruity or floral replacements we like: a sweeter rosé, pomelo or grapefruit liqueur, Lillet Blanc, or Domaine de Canton ginger liqueur.

The Group Chat

★ ★ ★

Mezcal is bold, Amaro Montenegro is bold, and they complement each other well here. Montenegro is produced in Italy and combines dozens of botanicals for this caramel-colored spirit with a bitter orange flavor. This one is strong, so make sure you sip rather than slurp—otherwise you'll be finding an excuse to stay home when your friends text you at 10 P.M. asking, "You ready to go?"

GLASS TYPE

[ROCKS]

INGREDIENTS

1½ ounces (45 ml) Banhez Mezcal Joven

1½ ounces (45 ml) Amaro Montenegro

Orange peel for garnish

DIRECTIONS

1. Pour the Banhez Mezcal Joven and Amaro Montenegro into a mixing glass.

2. Add ice and stir until the contents are completely integrated.

3. Strain into a rocks glass filled with ice.

4. Rub the orange peel around the rim of the glass to release its aromas, then drop it into the cocktail.

Judge Judy

 ★ ★ ★

Rhubarb liqueur's bright and tart flavors remind us of our favorite TV judge, an iconic Libra herself. Although the flavor is difficult to find here in the States, Giffard produces a delicious version that we balance out in this cocktail with citrus vodka and Luxardo. Also, if you're a fervent vodka drinker, we recommend trying out Ketel One's botanical collection, which includes flavors like grapefruit & rose or cucumber & mint. It's always a good idea to have some fun and light vodkas on hand to play around with (or to just keep on your bar cart so people think you're sophisticated).

GLASS TYPE

[ROCKS]

INGREDIENTS

1½ ounces (45 ml) Ketel One Citroen vodka

¾ ounce (23 ml) Giffard Rhubarb liqueur

¼ ounce (8 ml) Luxardo Maraschino liqueur

½ ounce (15 ml) lime juice

Lemon wheel for garnish

DIRECTIONS

1. Pour the Ketel One Citroen, Giffard Rhubarb, Luxardo, and lime juice into a cocktail shaker.

2. Add ice and shake vigorously.

3. Strain into a rocks glass filled with ice.

4. Garnish with a lemon wheel.

Lez Be Friends

★ ★ ★

We named this cocktail for mixy, gets-along-with-everyone Libras, balancing out the whiskey with the very sweet and bright pineapple. Pineapple is one of the juices that blend really well with whiskey, and we chose rye for this drink since the dryness is welcome here over the sweetness of a bourbon. Whiskey is something we recommend splurging a bit on if you can—Knob Creek rye is pricier than Old Overholt, but worth it if it fits in your budget.

GLASS TYPE

[COUPE]

INGREDIENTS

2 ounces (60 ml) Old Overholt rye

1½ ounces (45 ml) pineapple juice

½ ounce (15 ml) lemon juice

1 egg white

Amarena cherry for garnish

DIRECTIONS

1. Pour the Old Overholt rye, pineapple juice, and lemon juice into a cocktail shaker.

2. Add the egg white to the shaker.

3. First, do a dry shake (do not add any ice).

4. Add ice and shake again vigorously.

5. Strain into a chilled coupe glass.

6. Garnish with the Amarena cherry.

☾ NONALCOHOLIC VERSION

+ Omit the rye and use double the amount of pineapple juice, and add ½ ounce (15 ml) simple syrup (instructions on page 26) along with the other ingredients. First do a dry shake (do not add any ice). Add ice and shake again vigorously. Strain into a chilled coupe glass and garnish with an Amarena cherry.

Raw Egg Warning

Consuming raw or lightly cooked eggs poses a risk of food-borne illness.

Libra Night Life

While the countless degenerate hours we've spent on the dance floor stepping in unknown liquids are special and timeless, what would those nights really be without the precious personalities the universe has blessed us with in the communal club bathrooms? While ordering at the bar or getting the best spot in front of the DJ booth are battles often lost, the bathroom line and the bathroom itself are a social opportunity all of their own. To all the supportive strangers calling each other hot in the side-by-side sinks, sharing their Chanel eyeliner (or a literal fifty-cent spritz of Margiela perfume), you are the real MVPs. You're kind and loving while expecting nothing in return. Libras, you thrive in these hyper-social and sweet environments. Our tip to you is to embrace who you are and foster all the special connections you can because it's such a special skill.

This story is one of our favorite and most wholesome bathroom stories from Mood Ring. As a bartender, you develop an iron-clad bladder. On long weekend nights, we're on our feet from open to close, a full twelve hours. When things pick up around 10 P.M., that's our last bathroom break. Without being crass, it's like all of our pee is put in this time capsule and buried in the ground, and we can't open that thing up for six more hours. We have to hydrate enough not to pass out, and do shots of tequila (or, secretly, water) with our regulars. And once in a while, when the call of nature gets too urgent, we do have to ignore our thirsty customers for a bathroom break.

This one night, I cut the line during one of these breaks, and in the bathroom I saw a girl sitting on the ground crying. The crying part was, of course, alarming, but the real red flag was that this girl was in distressed denim SHORTS sitting on the floor in the bathroom of a club. That's one of those things you do when you're testing the limits of your immune system, not to mention your laundromat. I asked her if she was okay, and right at that moment another girl walked in and saw the crier and immediately said, "Girl, you good? Get your dumb ass off the ground! Don't you know there's literally pee everywhere?" The crying girl laughed and got up and the two girls walked off together hand in hand.

I relieved myself and got back to work. At closing time, I stepped outside to get some air and I noticed the two bathroom girls sitting on the bench outside. They're giggling, and one of them says to me, "Oh my god, you work here, right? You have to hear this story." So apparently this night was the first time these two had ever met, and I had witnessed the exact moment they met—in the bathroom. The girl was crying because she saw her ex at the bar and then immediately also lost her purse with her phone, wallet, house keys, everything. The other girl proceeded to pay for this girl's drinks after the bathroom rescue, and they hung out all night and they found out by chance that they grew up ten miles apart in Texas and have a bunch of mutual friends. By this point, apparently, they're new best friends. What happened next was some drunken Pixar-level wholesome shit. The crying girl (no longer crying, of course) said she was hungry, and without flinching, the other girl opened up her small purse, pulled out a bundle of aluminum foil, and unwrapped it to reveal a bacon, egg, and cheese on a roll. She fed it right into her new friend's mouth. Not one word was exchanged. They just sat there in silence as one fed and the other chewed. I nodded, wished them a good night, and walked away. Libras will create friendships anywhere, even in line for the club bathroom—we love that about you, and our tip is to keep spreading your light into the world. <3

SCORPIO

OCTOBER 23–NOVEMBER 21

Imagine a cauldron with a fire blazing underneath it and a stew brewing inside. If that stew were a Scorpio, it would be seasoned with intensity, mystery, moodiness, perceptiveness, and complexity. The one ingredient you never put in is fear. In any *Battle Royale*, *Hunger Games*, *Lord of the Flies*, or *Survivor* scenario, Scorpios will always come to win and take no prisoners. Never double-cross a Scorpio. Keanu Reeves as John Wick, seeking revenge for the murder of his dog, is Big. Scorpio. Energy.

Scorpio, underneath your mysterious and stoic façade lies a tumultuous emotional undercurrent that is honestly quite sensitive. You are hesitant to open up to others and will fight to avoid being misunderstood. You are the type to socialize only within a core group of friends, and you'll shun people who you consider to be randoms. You do get your fix of mingling, though, typically through the format of first dates and one-night stands. Your style is reminiscent of the female wolf spider, which will mate with a male spider and then kill and eat him. Scorpios have a reputation for getting mixed up in love affairs, but once you find that irresistible person you brand "The One," you will latch on as hard as you can and stay fiercely loyal. And that can happen anywhere from the dating app you swear you hate to a shared cigarette outside the dive bar.

IDEAL DATE for a SCORPIO

You've been flirting all week in your favorite language: the tease. You know, normal things like calling them capitalist pigs for owning cryptocurrency or spoiled because their parents still pay their cell phone bill (hey, Mom said it would be cheaper to be on the family plan). You tell them to meet you at the fancy candle store in the city. They're thinking $45 for a candle on a first date is certainly an interesting choice—and hot wax dripping on the chest could be a great date but might be more like date-number-three territory? And then you pull them into a phone booth inside the candle store—you know, one of those red British phone booths. So there you are, chest to chest with kind of a stranger. They're confused, but you confidently dial into the phone and say, "Hi, yes, table for two please." The phone booth opens up and you're in a dimly lit bar with velour seating, a sharply dressed man on piano, and bartenders with hand tattoos and cheekbones, the works. Yes, the *Martha Stewart Living*–worthy candle store to sexy speakeasy pipeline is a bit snobby. But snobby and sexy are words that might just be on your tombstone.

♡ YVES TUMOR, "Kerosene!"

♡ ALEX G, "SugarHouse" (Live)

♡ ME'SHELL NDEGÉOCELLO,
"If That's Your Boyfriend (He Wasn't Last Night)"

♡ MOLOKO, "Sing It Back"

♡ ANDRÉS, "You're Still the One"

♡ HEART, "Magic Man"

♡ JANET JACKSON, "I Get Lonely"

♡ ROOM 5, "Make Luv" (feat. Oliver Cheatham)

♡ CAMP LO, "Luchini AKA This Is It"

♡ CAROLINE POLACHEK, "Hit Me Where It Hurts"

OUR SCORPIO PLAYLIST

Wine Dine 69

★ ★ ★

The perfect date doesn't exis—

You know what we mean with this cocktail name. It wouldn't be Scorpio season without the smoky depth of mezcal, the grandfather of tequila. Here we've opted to use Union Uno Mezcal, which is on the more mellow side. If you're looking for something with a stronger smoky flavor, you can always ask your local liquor supplier for recommendations (we like Alipús San Andres or Madre Mezcal).

GLASS TYPE

[ROCKS]

INGREDIENTS

2 ounces (60 ml) Union Mezcal Uno

1¼ ounces (45 ml) orange juice

½ ounce (15 ml) ginger syrup (instructions on page 38)

2 drops Fee Brothers cardamom bitters

Star anise for garnish

DIRECTIONS

1. Pour the Union Mezcal Uno, orange juice, and ginger syrup into a cocktail shaker with ice.

2. Add two drops of cardamom bitters.

3. Give it a good shake.

4. Strain into a rocks glass filled with ice.

5. Garnish with an intact piece of star anise.

☾ NONALCOHOLIC VERSION

✦ Double the amount of orange juice and ginger syrup. Add two drops of cardamom bitters. Shake and strain into a rocks glass.

Nothing Was the Same

The name of this cocktail matches your dramatic Scorpio ass. The spiciness of the ginger beer with the 2-ounce (60-ml) liquor pour makes this one strong and bold. We recommend this cocktail if you're in the mood for something that's simple and quick to make. You can substitute the mango-flavored ginger beer with any other fruity flavor of your choice.

GLASS TYPE

[HIGHBALL]

INGREDIENTS

2 ounces (60 ml) Grey Goose vodka

½ ounce (15 ml) lemon juice

Mango-flavored ginger beer

Apricot for garnish

DIRECTIONS

1. Pour the Grey Goose and lemon juice into a cocktail shaker with ice.

2. Give it a good shake.

3. Strain into a highball glass filled with ice.

4. Top off with mango-flavored ginger beer.

5. Garnish with a piece of sliced apricot. (We sometimes use a piece of dried Turkish apricot.)

Sting

★ ★ ★

There are many ways to spice up your classic Margarita. You could go the route of infusion by soaking peppers (serrano or jalapeño) in your tequila, or try our favorite, throwing in some Ancho Reyes chile liqueur. This extra kick to the classic Margarita is exactly how we think of the intense Scorpio—not to be tamed. We have a salted rim on this one, but a Tajín rim works just as well if you're looking for an extra kick.

GLASS TYPE

[ROCKS]

INGREDIENTS

1½ ounces (45 ml) Espolòn Blanco tequila

½ ounce (15 ml) Ancho Reyes chile liqueur

½ ounce (15 ml) triple sec

½ ounce (15 ml) lime juice

Lime wedge for garnish

Salt (optional)

DIRECTIONS

1. Pour the Espolòn Blanco, Ancho Reyes, triple sec, and lime juice into a cocktail shaker.

2. Add ice and shake vigorously.

3. Strain into a rocks glass filled with ice. If you'd like a salt rim, before straining, squeeze a lime wedge around half of the rim of the rocks glass. Dip into salt to coat.

4. Garnish with the lime wedge.

Hearts on Fire

★ ★ ★

Like a Scorpio, this cocktail is dramatic, complex, and sexier than all the orgasms that happen on your block on Valentine's Day combined. Originally made by Carthusian monks in the South of France in the eighteenth century, Chartreuse has a strong herbal flavor with hints of honey, licorice, and saffron. The Italicus liqueur also adds a refreshing citrusy hint. If you don't manage to get the orgasm, you can always make a Hearts on Fire.

GLASS TYPE

[COUPE] OR
[NICK & NORA]

INGREDIENTS

1½ ounces (45 ml) Prairie Organic gin

1 ounce (30 ml) Italicus Bergamot liqueur or other light aperitif

½ ounce (15 ml) Yellow Chartreuse

½ ounce (15 ml) lime juice

Amarena cherry for garnish

DIRECTIONS

1. Pour the Prairie Organic, Italicus, Yellow Chartreuse, and lime juice into a cocktail shaker.

2. Add ice and shake vigorously.

3. Strain into a chilled coupe or Nick & Nora glass.

4. Garnish with the Amarena cherry.

Scorpio Night Life

There are certain things that are just bad for your health, like hitting a vape all day or cheating on a Scorpio—and yes, this is absolutely lifestyle advice. While getting revenge on a cheating ex spans the spectrum from ghosting them to taking a baseball bat to the windshield, this piece of advice for you Scorpios is about dealing with the rough nights we all have from time to time.

From behind the bar, we've witnessed our fair share of arguments and crying and even cheating (something our own friend did—sorry we had to include that). This story is about a young woman who had suspicions about her boyfriend cheating on her. This one weeknight we get a phone call at the bar, and the person on the other end is making unnecessary small talk, like "Hi, how's your night going," and "The weather's so gloomy today." We're trying to get her to get to the point of the call and she finally spits out that she thinks her boyfriend is cheating on her. They have their iPhone location sharing on, so she knows he's at Mood Ring and wants us to tell her if he's there with another girl. Part of our job as bartenders is to be like a vampire: stay in the shadows and out of people's business unless they invite you into the house. We were so shocked and tried not to laugh on the phone, not because we didn't feel for her but there was something so wild about getting a call from a stranger asking you to check if they're getting cheated on.

We responded by saying unfortunately we didn't feel comfortable providing that information, and if she wanted to find out she could maybe come to see for herself. She thanked us for our time and hung up. Now let me tell you, we don't know where she came from, but she pulled up like a parent when her kid gets suspended from school. She tiptoed through the front door breathing all heavy, and shyly walked up to the bar. Imagine what a twenty-something-year-old looks like when they're putting on a disguise but they only have ten minutes and can only use what's in their bedroom. She was wearing what looked to be a messy brunette wig with an oversized hoodie and a pair of NASCAR-branded sunglasses. In a soft voice she said, "Hey— is it cool if I look around?" We nodded. We had already looked around at the maybe fifteen people there that night and deduced which one had to be her boyfriend, and he happened to be sitting in the most secluded nook in the bar with another person. So we rushed from the bar toward our kitchen, where our security camera screens are, and saw the girl approach them. Mostly we wanted to make sure no one was getting punched in the face, but she merely walked briskly past the secluded nook, giving it a quick glance, pulled a 180, and strode back out the front door, never to be seen again (although honestly if she came back sans disguise, we would never have known).

While we realize the combination of alcohol and crowds of horny people don't always result in the best decisions, our advice for you intense Scorpios is to learn from this girl, take a step back, and evaluate situations clearly without the clouds of alcohol or the heat of passion making decisions for you. Clearly there were some trust issues with that relationship regardless of whether or not there was any cheating, but when it came down to it she got the information she needed, and we hope she and her wig are doing well.

SAGITTARIUS

NOVEMBER 22–DECEMBER 21

The average Sagittarian walks into a party and spends the first twenty minutes saying their hellos to all the people they know and chuckling every time a friend says, "Wait, you know _____?" The answer is: yes, you know everyone. Your adventurous nature is complemented by a deeply felt sense of optimism and positivity. This could manifest itself in your life in any number of ways: whether it means your passport keeps running out of pages or you've changed careers enough times your parents don't even care to keep track anymore. You believe that everything will work out in the end, so you're not afraid to make big moves that other signs might take years to contemplate and plan out. The one thing you never want to feel is trapped, and you would always rather take that big leap of faith. What's the worst that could happen?

You're not scared of anything, which leads to incredible opportunities in your personal and professional life. You have a tramp stamp tattoo that says "carpe diem" in gothic-style lettering, and not in an ironic way. You deserve a lover who won't hold you back from all your curiosities, from taking glass-blowing classes to threesomes—and when you fall for someone, it's often deep and quick. Doesn't eloping sound romantic? But remember, even amongst the chaos that you thrive in, stability can be sexy too. Don't forget to follow through on your big ideas.

IDEAL DATE
for a SAGITTARIUS

The ideal date for a Sagittarius is an exercise in Google Calendar-ing, which doesn't sound so hot but it is. At 1 P.M. is your coffee date—something casual to get to know a person without anything getting misconstrued. Now it's 4 P.M., and you meet your second date at the park where they've prepared a nice little picnic spread. Just in time to soak up the coffee from date one. This one seems a bit overeager, but they put in the effort and definitely have potential. Moving on to your 7 P.M. date, a nice dinner and cocktail moment. This is actually the one you're most excited for, and you definitely planned for the sun to be setting on your face as the entrées come out. You chat and have a lovely time. The date went great, and you plan a second one on the spot. Date one to explore the personality, date two to explore the underwear. In a way this is like a reverse sports draft, where the top prospects are saved for the last of the night. So then you have your final date at 11 P.M. Drinks, and you take them home. Serious relationship potential? Probably not, but they're hot, and sometimes that's enough. So really, your perfect date is just an exercise in ordering everything on the menu.

♡ LIZZY MERCIER DESCLOUX, "Fire"

♡ CLAIRO, "Softly"

♡ SUSUMU YOKOTA, "Sexy Planet"

♡ GRAND PUBA, "I Like It
(I Wanna Be Where You Are)"

♡ THE STROKES, "You Only Live Once"

♡ STEREOLAB, "Pack Yr Romantic Mind"

♡ D. TIFFANY, "Get Back to You Soon"

♡ GIRLS, "Lust for Life"

♡ THE GAME, "Hate It or Love It" (feat. 50 Cent)

♡ OKAY KAYA, "Believe"

OUR SAGITTARIUS PLAYLIST

Sorry I Ghosted You

★ ★ ★

It's okay, we've all been on both sides of the ghosting equation, Sagittarius or not—though they are notorious culprits of it. Here we have a calming and soothing concoction for Sagittarius's winter season, using honey syrup and one of our absolute favorite liqueurs, the Williams pear from Pür•likör. If you have difficulty finding their brand, we also like American Fruits and St. George pear liqueurs.

GLASS TYPE

[ROCKS]

INGREDIENTS

1 ounce (30 ml) Espolòn Blanco tequila

1½ ounces (45 ml) Pür•likör Williams or other pear liqueur

¼ ounce (8 ml) honey syrup

½ ounce (15 ml) lemon juice

Cinnamon stick for garnish

recipe continues

DIRECTIONS

1. Pour the Espolòn Blanco tequila, Pür•likör, honey syrup, and lemon juice into a cocktail shaker. The honey syrup is very sweet, so make sure you don't overpour.

2. Add ice and shake vigorously.

3. Strain into a rocks glass filled with ice.

4. Garnish with the cinnamon stick.

MAKING HONEY SYRUP:

+ In a bowl, combine equal parts honey and hot water. Transfer the mixture to a bottle and store in the fridge for up to 6 months.

Super Rush

Is the title of this cocktail a poppers reference? That's between you and your bodega guy. For those long nights out on the town that Sagittarius is so fond of, we present a Red Bull cocktail. If you're feeling *very* fancy and have a half hour to make a cocktail, we love this one served out of a carved pineapple.

GLASS TYPE

[HIGHBALL]

INGREDIENTS

1½ ounces (45 ml) Goslings Black Seal Rum

1 ounce (30 ml) Combier Crème de Pêche de Vigne or other peach liqueur

1½ ounces (45 ml) pineapple juice

Red Bull

Lime wedge for garnish

DIRECTIONS

1. Pour the Goslings, Combier, and pineapple juice into a cocktail shaker.

2. Add ice and shake vigorously.

3. Strain into a highball glass filled with ice.

4. Top off with Red Bull. (This is not a paid advertisement, but the tropical Yellow Edition Red Bull is a great upgrade here, too.)

5. Garnish with the lime wedge.

Fallen Angels

★ ★ ★

The sinning angel: this cocktail is a reference to one of our favorite Wong Kar-wai films, *Fallen Angels*. The ending scene shows an attractive couple riding a motorcycle through a tunnel, a cigarette hanging off the man's lips, as you hear the woman's narration: "The road home isn't very long, and I know I'll be getting off soon. But at this moment, I'm feeling such lovely warmth"—and what could be more Sagittarius than that? This was one of our most popular cocktails concocted by bartender Randall Morris. The floral hibiscus is a great partner to the tart flavor of the tamarind, and the black peppercorn adds a nice depth to the cocktail as well.

GLASS TYPE

[ROCKS]

INGREDIENTS

1¼ ounces (45 ml) hibiscus-infused Tito's vodka (instructions follow)

1¼ ounces (45 ml) tamarind nectar

½ ounce (15 ml) black peppercorn syrup (instructions on page 93)

½ ounce (15 ml) lemon juice

Dried orange for garnish

recipe continues

DIRECTIONS

1. Pour the hibiscus-infused Tito's, tamarind, black peppercorn syrup, and lemon juice into a cocktail shaker.

2. Add ice and shake vigorously.

3. Strain into a rocks glass filled with ice.

4. Garnish with the dried orange.

☾ MAKING HIBISCUS-INFUSED VODKA

✦ Pour a bottle of vodka (1 L) into an empty container, ideally another bottle or something with an easy-pour spout. Save the original bottle.

✦ Add ½ cup (18 g) dried hibiscus flowers and let sit for 8 hours, then check for flavor. If you want it stronger, leave it for another few hours, until desired flavor is achieved. (If you're in an absolute rush, you can bottle the hibiscus with the vodka and shake vigorously for a minute. It won't be fully infused, but you'll get the color and flavor from the hibiscus.)

✦ Strain into the original bottle, taking care to ensure that all of the flowers are separated out.

☾ NONALCOHOLIC VERSION

✦ Make a hibiscus-infused simple syrup: In a small saucepan over medium heat, combine 1 cup (240 ml) water, 1 cup (200 g) sugar, and ½ cup (18 g) dried hibiscus flowers. Simmer 10 minutes, continuously stirring in circles around the edge of the pot, until the sugar is completely dissolved. Let cool completely, then strain into a glass bottle or jar. Seal tightly and store in the fridge for up to 1 month.

✦ For the cocktail, double the amount of tamarind nectar and add ¾ ounce (23 ml) hibiscus syrup and the usual measurements of the other ingredients. Shake and strain into a rocks glass filled with ice.

Butterfly Effect

★ ★ ★

This cocktail is for the sexy Sags who theoretically want the full Lewis-and-Clark-lost-in-the-woods experience but really only want to go glamping. A riff on the classic Manhattan cocktail, this one's meant to be sipped. Zirbenz Stone Pine liqueur has a deep aromatic profile and, combined with bourbon, will convince you you're sniffing a tree in rural Oregon. The lavender twig adds a nice floral scent to finish out the cocktail.

GLASS TYPE

[ROCKS]

INGREDIENTS

Sugar

3 drops lavender bitters

2 ounces (60 ml) Maker's Mark bourbon

1½ ounces (45 ml) Zirbenz stone pine liqueur or other pine liqueur

½ ounce (15 ml) Dolin sweet vermouth

Dried lavender twig for garnish

DIRECTIONS

1. In a mixing glass, add a bar spoon of sugar and the lavender bitters.

2. Pour in the Maker's Mark, Zirbenz, and Dolin.

3. Add ice and stir.

4. Strain into a rocks glass filled with ice.

5. Garnish with the dried lavender twig.

Sagittarius Night Life

Back before ghosting via text was a thing, you'd just do it in real life at a bar like a normal person. Whether with a friend or a date, you'd just walk right out the door and not look back. To all you Sagittarians, we're sorry to say, but you're the Olympic medalists of ghosting. It's not always intentional, but you just get so excited and distracted by all the other things (and people) you want to do that night. So this tip is to help you avoid leaving your friend with that very specific and lonely feeling of barfing alone in the club bathroom because your flighty ass ditched them at the bar.

On one hot summer night, one of our barbacks let us know that a customer was feeling sick. We hurried over to the couch where this person was slumped over. She was with two of her friends, who seemed to be taking care of her. We provided her with some water and managed to move her to the outside bench for some fresh air. Her friends said she'd be okay, so we stepped back inside to get back to our jobs. After maybe thirty minutes, we sent one of the staff to check on her outside. Her friends were gone, and she was slumped over again by herself. Our barback stayed with her, making sure she was awake and hydrating, as another thirty minutes passed. At this point, we were worried she might have had things in her system beyond just liquor. I checked in with our staff, and no one remembered serving her drinks.

So we looked in her bag to see if her phone was there so we could contact someone, and what do you know, there was a half-empty bottle of rum and a couple small baggies of that good stuff. If there's one thing about the American healthcare system it's that it costs a lot of money to stay alive, and an ambulance is just an overpriced Uber XL half the time. So we checked her wallet first, and luckily she had health insurance. We called her an ambulance, and they took her away on a stretcher.

The next day we got a call—the man on the line started yelling, immediately calling us assholes, threatening to sue for overserving his daughter and sending her to the hospital. We explained what happened and that we didn't serve her any drinks, and he just yelled, "Fuck you," and hung up. A few minutes later we got another call. This time it was the girl herself, who apologized about her father and thanked us for taking care of her. She had no recollection of the night before, and all we could tell her about it was: "You need some better friends."

To be fair to Sags, you can make great friends because your passion can make you extremely loyal. But let this tale serve as a lesson: don't let your sometimes fickle mind and heart lead you to selfish decisions, and definitely don't forget to keep an eye on those who need you the most.

CAPRICORN

DECEMBER 22–JANUARY 19

One of the most ambitious and hard-working signs, Capricorns imbue an intensity in everything they do, and that's why they're known as the workaholic sign. Capricorn, you can't shake that drive, whether you're in a Patagonia vest on Wall Street doing lines under your desk all night or in your studio drop-kicking easels because the composition isn't just right. After spending years in your life, your friends are still unsure whether they've actually ever seen you sleep. In everything that you do, you're all in.

In friendship, you seek people who can appreciate your ambition and build a relationship on mutual respect. You keep a busy schedule, though, so you surround yourself with others who also have a lot going on—you do pick up the habits of those around you, after all. Those who can't keep up the pace or aren't invested in their own futures will tend to escape your interest.

In love, you're tough to catch. You're pragmatic and hate to waste time, so why invest emotionally in something or someone when you're not 100 percent sure? At the very least, though, practice makes perfect, and you're excellent in bed. In the boudoir, as in all things, you're motivated by purpose, so continue to chase after the things that drive you. Just don't forget to let yourself fall in love once in a while. It's good for you.

IDEAL DATE for a CAPRICORN

You meet your date at the sexiest time and place possible: 12 P.M. on a Wednesday at the Australian coffee shop near your job. When you told your date this, they were extremely confused, but hey, you're attractive as hell and your personality isn't half bad either, so they're rolling with it. You get a flat white and start conducting your ~~interview~~ date. *Income?* Mostly to make sure you can go to the same restaurants and bars without money being an issue. *Pets?* Cat person or dog person, never both—people need to make up their damn minds. *Relationship with mother?* Your therapist told you it matters. *Big spoon or little spoon?* Sleep, when you actually partake, is sacred. Thirty-one minutes later, your lunch break is over and you approve of their responses. You decide that if someone is this attractive in broad daylight it's worth checking out how they look after a couple cocktails in the horny red light of your favorite bar. You get up and say, "This can work. I'll reach out in three to five business days for next steps."

♡ LES SINS, "Grind"

♡ ESG, "Dance"

♡ KAMAIYAH, "I'm On"

♡ SHINICHIRO YOKOTA, "Do it Again"

♡ JANET JACKSON, "No Sleeep"

♡ BLOOD ORANGE, "Champagne Coast"

♡ GUCCI MANE, "Lemonade"

♡ ABBA, "Gimme! Gimme! Gimme!
(A Man After Midnight)"

♡ BRAIDS, "Young Buck" (DJ Python Remix)

♡ LOS ÁNGELES AZULES, "Nunca Es Suficiente"
(feat. Natalia Lafourcade)

OUR CAPRICORN PLAYLIST

Call Me Daddy

You Capricorns are type A, on the far end of the power spectrum, and we love you for it. Especially this one customer who came in and ordered a drink, and when it was time to pay, she just snapped her fingers and cash appeared from below. We peeked over the bar and her sub was on a leash on all fours handing her cash whenever she asked for it. That's a Call-Me-Daddy move.

GLASS TYPE

[ROCKS]

INGREDIENTS

2 ounces (60 ml) Espolòn Añejo tequila

½ ounce (15 ml) Cointreau triple sec

¾ ounce (23 ml) tart cherry juice

½ ounce (15 ml) lime juice

Dried lime wheel for garnish

DIRECTIONS

1. Pour the Espolòn Añejo, Cointreau, cherry juice, and lime juice into a cocktail shaker.

2. Add ice and shake vigorously.

3. Strain into a rocks glass filled with ice.

4. Garnish with the dried lime wheel.

The Dominatrix

★ ★ ★

We use one of our favorite beers, Tsingtao, which is a light lager, for our adaptation of the classic Michelada. We recommend this cocktail during brunch or whenever you're craving a savory drink. This is two full drinks in one for you multitasking Capricorns. And chugging vodka with Worcestershire sauce will give you the spanking that only Capricorns can take without flinching.

(Please note that Clamato juice is not vegan.)

GLASS TYPE

[HIGHBALL]

INGREDIENTS

1½ ounces (45 ml) Ketel One vodka

3 ounces (90 ml) Clamato juice

½ ounce (15 ml) lime juice

2 drops Worcestershire sauce

Tajín Clásico seasoning

Tsingtao lager

Lime wedge for garnish

DIRECTIONS

1. Pour the Ketel One, Clamato, lime juice, and Worcestershire sauce into a cocktail shaker.

2. Add ice and shake vigorously.

3. Rim the highball glass with Tajín (see page 81).

4. Strain into a highball glass filled with ice.

5. Top off with Tsingtao lager.

6. Garnish with the lime wedge.

Something About Us

★ ★ ★

We absolutely love playing with activated charcoal, partly because it adds a bit of texture but mainly because it turns cocktails black. When built with edible gold or silver stars on top, this cocktail looks like a little galaxy in a rocks glass—just as full of potential as you powerful Caps.

GLASS TYPE

[ROCKS]

INGREDIENTS

1¼ ounces (45 ml) Espolòn Blanco tequila

¾ ounce (23 ml) grapefruit juice

½ ounce (15 ml) pineapple juice

Splash of lime juice

Splash of simple syrup (instructions on page 26)

Touch of activated charcoal (or a few drops of food coloring)

Edible stars for garnish

DIRECTIONS

1. Pour the Espolòn Blanco, grapefruit juice, pineapple juice, lime juice, and simple syrup into a cocktail shaker.

2. Add a whisper of activated charcoal powder. You can always add more if you want a darker color, but start with a little first.

3. Add ice and shake vigorously.

4. Strain into a rocks glass filled with ice.

5. Garnish with a sprinkle of edible stars.

☾ NONALCOHOLIC VERSION

✦ Substitute the tequila with double the amount of grapefruit and pineapple juice and use the same amounts of all other ingredients. Shake and strain into a rocks glass filled with ice. Garnish with edible stars.

Open Up the Pit

★ ★ ★

We wouldn't feel right not featuring White Label Yerba Mate—a caffeinated bottled drink that helps keep our stretch of Brooklyn energized enough to dance until the wee hours of the morning—in one of our Capricorn cocktails. If you're in a rush, take a big gulp of Yerba Mate, throw the ingredients straight into the bottle, place your thumb on top, flip it over and back, and there you have it: the cheating on the SATs version of this cocktail.

GLASS TYPE

[COUPE] OR
[NICK & NORA]

INGREDIENTS

1½ ounces (45 ml) Prairie Organic gin

1½ ounces (45 ml) Domaine de Canton ginger liqueur

½ ounce (15 ml) Dolin dry vermouth

White Label Yerba Mate or other yerba mate (we also like Club Mate)

Rosemary sprig for garnish

DIRECTIONS

1. Pour the Prairie Organic, Domaine de Canton, and Dolin into a cocktail shaker.

2. Add ice and shake vigorously.

3. Strain into a chilled coupe glass.

4. Top with a splash of White Label Yerba Mate.

5. Garnish with the rosemary sprig.

Capricorn Night Life

Capricorns are the ones driving up the view counts on motivational videos on YouTube. You know the ones, where someone is talking about wanting to be successful as much as they want to breathe, set to the *300* soundtrack, or our personal favorite, a video of Shuzo Matsuoka, a Japanese former professional tennis player, yelling out, "Never Give Up!" while fishing for Asiatic clams. Some people go hard or go home—you're the type to go hard and then just keep going hard. There's some joke about taking two Viagras here, but we won't make it.

Capricorns work hard and party hard—we see you all showing up to the club at 3 A.M. asking for vodka Red Bulls and sneaking off every few minutes to the bathroom with your friend and then coming back giggling and wiping your noses. We love the spiral, but dammit, take care of yourself too, please.

This story is about a person who decided to let loose and learned there is such a thing as too loose. It was one of our harder techno parties and Mood Ring was slammed—we're talking multiple drink orders back-to-back-to-back and only taking water breaks as we simultaneously closed out tabs. As we handed someone their drink, we saw one of the party promoters waving his hand with a bewildered look on his face. He said, "Someone needs medical attention." We ask what happened. He says, "I don't know, look at this guy." He points at a tall man—like power-forward-in-the-NBA tall, or can't-fit-into-a-Porsche tall—walking up with his hand wrapped in his white T-shirt, soaked in blood. We say, "What happened?!" The man's face was completely calm as he said, "I don't really know. Well, okay, I was trying to spin the disco ball and then I think I cut myself a little." He showed us his hand, and it looked like he had stuck it in a bag of literal shards of glass. (Hey, it happens from time to time.) We asked if he wanted us to call someone to get him to a hospital. He said he was fine. We said, "Sorry, but we can't have you bleeding all over the place, and you might need stitches." He nodded reasonably, said, "I understand," and casually walked out into the night. Hope he's doing okay, wherever he is.

At the end of the night, we checked the camera footage and found that the man had been jumping up and down on the dance floor, slapping the disco ball and spinning it. He had damaged he disco ball, which had tiny pieces of mirror broken off all over it and looked almost as bad as his hand. That was the last night we ever had a disco ball.

So to all you Caps out there: we want you to achieve your dreams as badly as you do, but *please* eat your veggies, get some sleep every night, sip rather than chug your liquor, and avoid shiny, sharp objects at all costs.

AQUARIUS

JANUARY 20–FEBRUARY 18

Oh, Aquarius. You are the rebels who live life in your own lane, and let's be honest, it doesn't really matter to you what others might think. So what if your Hello Kitty plush collection stays on the bed during sex? Or you wake up in the morning with your body saying please take care of me and reward it with a cigarette and a cold brew? You might very well be on your second iPhone of the last six months because you lose everything, but at least you had a lot of fun doing it. (Sidebar—the lost and found at bars is often fascinating: clothes, phones, drugs, journals, international passports, and one time, a prosthetic leg.)

As an Aquarian, you're the walking billboard for the phrase, "I'm built DIFFERENT." You're sharp and intelligent, and you look for the same in a potential partner. When in bed with an Aquarius, skip all the standard dirty talk and whisper in their ear, "I respect your boundaries." They will get chills as hairs rise on the back of their neck, because nothing is hotter to an Aquarius than boundaries. You like dating someone who has their own friends and own hobbies and can give you space when you need it. You can be a difficult person to deal with as a friend and a lover because you love to deflect. Giving up personal information or, god forbid, being emotionally vulnerable are just not on the menu with you. But people are drawn in by your mystery, your blasé attitude, and your brilliance. When you meet someone who understands you and deserves you, don't be afraid to let them get a taste. It'll be worth their while—and yours.

IDEAL DATE
for an AQUARIUS

You wake up from your post-dinner nap at 10 P.M.—really the perfect hour to pregame those espresso Martinis you've been thinking about. You meet your date at a dive bar, then move over to the cocktail bar, then to the club. But by this point it's 4 A.M. and the club is closed. Time to go ho—just kidding, the night is only halfway done. You end up in the industrial part of town at a warehouse that looks like it might be a recycling plant by day. But the pounding techno music and the leather-clad strangers swaying back and forth give the game away. You dance at the rave until the sun rises outside the window. In the shared car home, in your raspy end-of-the-night-Christian-Bale-as-Batman voice, you ask to plug into the aux because you need something with a hot BPM. You casually open the window and projectile vomit at 30 mph as your date looks on, impressed. You wipe your mouth, apply some eye drops, and mentally prepare notes for the big meeting at your whole-ass job you're about to go to. You gaze out the window as Vanessa Carlton's "A Thousand Miles" plays softly in the background. *Making my way downtown . . .*

♡ LE TIGRE, "Deceptacon"

♡ MR. FINGERS, "Amnesia"

♡ FAYE WONG, "Heart of Glass" (Live)

♡ TRAVIS SCOTT, "Coordinate"

♡ CHAKA KHAN, "Like Sugar"

♡ NEW FOUND GLORY, "My Friends Over You"

♡ THE BLAZE, "Territory"

♡ MONDO GROSSO, "ラビリンス（Labyrinth）"

♡ ELISAPIE, "Navvaatara"

♡ BAD BUNNY, "Solo de Mi"

OUR AQUARIUS PLAYLIST

What's My Age Again?

★ ★ ★

We love a classic Malibu with pineapple juice, so just think of this as a more fun, upgraded version. We know that juicing oranges may seem like an unnecessary extra step, but here the taste of fresh juice combined with the added texture is worth it. This is for all you young-at-heart and/or young-in-reality Aquarians who aren't scared of a sugar hangover. Is *hangover* even a real word, anyway?

GLASS TYPE

[ROCKS]

INGREDIENTS

1 teaspoon sugar

3 basil leaves

1 ounce (30 ml) Malibu Original coconut rum

1 ounce (30 ml) Goslings Black Seal Rum

2 ounces (60 ml) fresh-squeezed orange juice

DIRECTIONS

1. Put the sugar and basil leaves into your cocktail shaker and muddle.

2. Next, pour the Malibu, Goslings, and orange juice into the shaker.

3. Add ice and give it a good shake.

4. Pour all the contents of the shaker directly into your rocks glass, top off with ice as needed, and garnish with basil leaf.

☾ NONALCOHOLIC VERSION

✦ This is a seriously refreshing drink even without the rum. Follow the same instructions to muddle the sugar and basil leaves, and double the amount of orange juice.

THE COCKTAILS

Pepsi Nail

★ ★ ★

Pepsi and its many . . . alternatives, while not our favorite, are some of the fun things you indulge in when you're young (they say Pepsi is for those who think young, after all), or in Las Vegas, or both. This cocktail is both fun and classy, balancing the two like the complexities of an Aquarius. The Combier Liqueur de Violette adds a nice floral flavor to the cocktail as well as, get this, a pretty violet color. We're huge fans of the Korean soda Milkis (especially the strawberry and melon flavors), which features some of the cutest soda artwork around, and adds some nice bubbles to this cocktail, just like Pepsi and Pepsi alternatives.

GLASS TYPE

[COUPE]

INGREDIENTS

2 ounces (60 ml) Grey Goose vodka

½ ounce (15 ml) Combier Liqueur de Violette

½ ounce (15 ml) lemon juice

Milkis Strawberry soda

Strawberry for garnish

DIRECTIONS

1. Pour the Grey Goose, Combier, and lemon juice into a cocktail shaker.

2. Add ice and give it a good shake.

3. Strain into a coupe glass.

4. Top off with Milkis Strawberry soda.

5. Halve a strawberry and place it on a cocktail skewer, a toothpick, or on the rim for garnish.

One-Night Stand

★ ★ ★

This cocktail is for those wild and spontaneous nights you go home with a stranger for one reason and that reason is "Why not?" Thanks to these nights, you know exactly how much a plan B and a Gatorade costs, and they're also the reason you have an extensive hoodie collection. So here's to all the hoodies that smell like people you won't ever see again, except maybe one time from across the Greek yogurt section at Whole Foods and you pretend not to notice. Sorry, just had a flashback. Back to the cocktail!

There are many different combinations of peppers and liquors that you can try infusing, and the great thing is that you can control how spicy you want to make it. Bird's eye chile pepper is common in many Southeast Asian cuisines, and here we've chosen it to infuse our favorite Espolòn Blanco tequila. If you can't find bird's eye chiles, another pepper like serrano will do just fine. And we also love using Hornitos tequila, which is at a slightly cheaper price point but just as smooth. The Aperol adds a subtle bitterness to this cocktail, so feel free to experiment with something sweet like a fruit liqueur if that's more your taste. Like any good Aquarius cocktail, this one is predicated on adaptability.

GLASS TYPE

[HIGHBALL]

INGREDIENTS

2 ounces (60 ml) bird's eye chile-infused Espolòn Blanco tequila (instructions follow)

½ ounce (15 ml) Aperol

½ ounce (15 ml) lime juice

Seltzer

Bird's eye chile pepper for garnish

DIRECTIONS

1. Pour the bird's eye chile–infused Espolòn Blanco, Aperol, and lime juice into a cocktail shaker.

2. Add ice and give it a good shake.

3. Strain into a highball glass filled with ice.

4. Top off with seltzer.

5. Garnish with a bird's eye chile pepper.

MAKING CHILE-INFUSED TEQUILA:

+ Use 2 bird's eye chili peppers per 1-liter bottle of Espolòn Blanco tequila. Cut open the peppers, add them to the bottle, and let them steep for 10 minutes, then check periodically until you're at your desired flavor level.

+ You can make it as spicy as you would like. Feel free to add more peppers or let it steep for longer, and just taste test it frequently to find your favorite balance. Once you're happy with the spiciness level, strain into a separate bottle.

Young, Dumb, and Full of Rum

★ ★ ★

We were once given a bottle of Hana makgeolli by a good friend, and we've kept a bottle of it stocked at home ever since. Makgeolli is a low-ABV rice wine from Korea, and the one produced by Brooklyn-based Hana is seriously delicious on its own. We like to pair it with different liquors based on the alcohol content, and here we suggest using rum, but you can also try experimenting with something else, like mezcal. There's always fierce debate on honeydew vs. cantaloupe, and we love both, but the slightly sweeter honeydew works better in this particular cocktail. You can find honeydew juice at some specialty stores, or you can juice it yourself. This cocktail is fun, and busting out a rare makgeolli is the type of rebellion that Aquarius is known for.

GLASS TYPE

[ROCKS]

INGREDIENTS

2 ounces (60 ml) Hana makgeolli or a Nigori sake

1 ounce (30 ml) El Dorado white rum

1½ ounces (45 ml) honeydew juice

½ ounce (15 ml) lime juice

Honeydew square for garnish

DIRECTIONS

1. Pour the Hana makgeolli, El Dorado, honeydew juice, and lime juice into a cocktail shaker.

2. Add ice and give it a good shake.

3. Strain into a rocks glass filled with ice.

4. Place the honeydew square on a toothpick or skewer for garnish.

Aquarius Night Life

Aquarians are those who live their lives as they say in the classic series *The Fast and the Furious* a quarter mile at a time—nothing else matters. Therefore, the ungodly and reckless things that occur in club bathrooms are peak Aquarian maneuvers. It's true when they say that when it rains it pours, and when there's destruction to our bathrooms it comes in pairs, and even occasionally triplets.

As a play on our name Mood Ring, our bathroom walls are adorned with decorative plates, and custom printed, each plate is a celebrity along with a photo of a ring that we feel matches the personality of that celebrity. The plate that always gets stolen and has to be replaced is the one of Paris Hilton wearing her infamous T-shirt that reads: *Got Blow?*

One busy weekend night, we got word that one of our toilets was not flushing properly, which is always a downer. We'd rather get spit on—in the face—by a stranger than deal with overflowing toilets. We went to investigate and found that the toilet had a weak flush and therefore was clogging. But even more alarming was what we found right next to the toilet: the sink had been broken off the wall. Realistically, the only way that happens is when someone puts a whole lot of weight on it, like, let's say, I don't know, someone sits on it, possibly with rhythmic motion and force. And to top it all off, our Paris Hilton plate was missing again. We looked around, connecting the dots like we were detectives and the Louvre had just been robbed. We pieced together that people (plural) must have been fucking on the sink, broke it, stole our Paris Hilton plate, and disappeared into the night. The perfect crime.

We couldn't figure out the issue with the weak flushing toilet, so we hired a plumber the next day, who was confused as well. He removed the toilet from the floor, flipped the whole chunk of porcelain, grabbed his pliers, and managed to remove the obstruction. Lo and behold, it was a coat hanger someone tried to flush. Now, we don't know that the culprit was an Aquarius, but all the signs point that way. Peak Aquarius is do now, ask questions later, and we love them for that (usually). What's not to love about someone who has sex in a club bathroom, breaks the sink, steals a plate, and flushes a coat hanger down the toilet all in one night? That's a friend you absolutely keep around for laughs. Maybe not for advice, though. They can break some hearts or they can break some sinks, but they can't do all that *and* fix your problems. Don't get greedy.

PISCES

FEBRUARY 19–MARCH 20

When you graduate from Heartbreak University, with your brain scrambled into eggs and thrown across the pavement, all you can do is wander around trying to collect the pieces. Sorry to be dramatic, but when you're in the fog of heartache it really does feel like that. You just want to go back home but you don't know the way, and you look to the person who broke your heart for direction but there's none to be found. A wise Piscean friend of ours once counseled when we were going through something like this, "The only way out of hell is to crawl." So we crawl.

As a Pisces, you live with your head blissfully in the clouds and might even come off as aloof because you just can't be pulled down to Earth. When you care about someone, though, you love to share your tissues and your Criterion Channel login. But be careful: your emotional generosity can sometimes attract people who just want to use you to solve their own problems.

Beyond your ridiculous Kleenex budget, you're also an original and a daydreamer. Many creative geniuses are born under this sign. When it comes to love, you're a sucker for big romantic gestures, like your lover flying coach across continents to see you on your birthday or maybe a flash-mob Bruno Mars marriage proposal at the mall if you're into that kind of thing. If you fall in love, it will be an engrossing part of your life and it will become an important part of who you are. This is why it is crucial to find someone who will fulfill all your emotional desires and can continue to make you feel appreciated while also allowing you to immerse yourself in your vivid inner life. But don't let your sensitivity build up unnecessary insecurities. Yes, it is possible for someone to love you AND forget to pick up your favorite green tea mochi from Trader Joe's. Try to remember that and the rest will fall into place.

IDEAL DATE for a PISCES

It's a calm night, and you and your date have your comfy pants on with nothing up top. This is a free-the-nip zone. Your date looks you in the eyes from across the room and says, "Is this okay?" as they set the needle on a vinyl record that's *exactly* what you want to hear because it reminds you of nice times from years ago. You're kneading dough in candle-light because you're a barefoot-listening-to-Solange-making-handmade-pasta type of Pisces. As you're moving the rolling pin back and forth, rain clattering outside in the dangerous world, your date comes up behind you and tucks their chin over your shoulder. It's called body contact, baby, and someone should really look into this power as renewable energy. You take in each other's scents like the dogs that you are and all of a sudden you're making love all over the unmade pasta, flour everywhere, kitchen utensils slipping to the ground. What a dirty mess we've made.

♡ MASSIVE ATTACK, "The Spoils"
(feat. Hope Sandoval)

♡ CHAZ BUNDICK MEETS THE MATTSON 2, "JBS"

♡ THE JESUS & MARY CHAIN, "Darklands"

♡ SEVDALIZA, "Marilyn Monroe"

♡ ROD WAVE, "Heart on Ice"

♡ AIR, "How Does It Make You Feel?"

♡ SOKO, "I'll Kill Her"

♡ WASHED OUT, "Feel It All Around"

♡ CHARLI XCX, "Stay Away"

♡ LUCY DACUS, "Night Shift"

OUR PISCIS PLAYLIST

As Tears Go By

★ ★ ★

Oh, intuitive and emotionally intelligent Pisces, just remember to wipe away your own tears before you offer your powers to others. Go ahead and use that spa coupon your aunt gave you—you deserve it. And afterward, when you're feeling refreshed, turn that big heart outward with this cocktail in hand.

We've deployed the Italicus Bergamot for another cocktail in this book because we love its complex herbal and citrus combo. It's an Italian liqueur originally from the nineteenth century, and it was called the "drink of kings." We like pairing it with a dry prosecco; the rosemary sprig rounds it off with a refreshing scent.

GLASS TYPE

[WINE]

INGREDIENTS

2 ounces (60 ml) Italicus Bergamot liqueur

½ ounce (15 ml) lemon juice

Prosecco

Rosemary sprig for garnish

DIRECTIONS

1. Pour the Italicus and lemon juice into a cocktail shaker.

2. Add ice and shake vigorously.

3. Strain into a wine glass with 3 ice cubes.

4. Top off with prosecco.

5. Garnish with the rosemary sprig.

Catfish

★ ★ ★

The idealist Pisces is a prime Catfish target, sorry to say. You look for the best in others and sometimes miss the red flag thrown on the forty-yard line (we're 75 percent sure this is a valid football reference).

We were recently introduced to Moshi Yuzu soda, which features yuzu oil to make a seriously delicious beverage. Here it's paired with gin and peach liqueur for a light and refreshing cocktail. If you can't find this particular brand, it's definitely fine to experiment with what you can find at your local Japanese grocery store or online. We recommend opting for something that isn't too sweet, as the Combier Pêche de Vigne does a good job of adding sweetness to the cocktail's flavor profile. The Swedish fish is our wink to cute Pisces, but it does harden a bit over the cold ice, so take your time with it rather than chomping away. And take your time giving those Tinder matches a thorough Google before you mentally plan your wedding too.

recipe continues

GLASS TYPE

[HIGHBALL]

INGREDIENTS

1½ ounces (45 ml) Prairie Organic gin

½ ounce (15 ml) Combier Crème de Pêche de Vigne

Moshi Yuzu sparkling drink

Mint for garnish

Swedish fish for garnish

DIRECTIONS

1. Pour the Prairie Organic and Combier into a cocktail shaker.

2. Add ice and shake vigorously.

3. Strain into a highball glass filled with ice.

4. Top off with Moshi Yuzu.

5. Place a mint leaf on the palm of your hand and spank it to release the aroma before using it to garnish the cocktail.

6. For a special Pisces touch, add an additional garnish of one or two Swedish fish on a cocktail skewer.

Heartbreak University

★ ★ ★

After you get your bachelor's in pain from Heartbreak University, you go right into Heartbreak Grad School. This cocktail is our classy take on the Martini to go with all of your heartbreak degrees. In our opinion, Tito's is the best bang for your buck, but Grey Goose is also a solid vodka choice if it's in your budget.

GLASS TYPE

[COUPE]

INGREDIENTS

2 ounces (60 ml) Grey Goose vodka

½ ounce (15 ml) Dolin dry vermouth

¾ ounce (23 ml) blueberry syrup

Lemon peel for garnish

DIRECTIONS

1. Pour the Grey Goose, Dolin, and blueberry syrup into a cocktail shaker.

2. Add ice and shake vigorously.

3. Strain into a chilled coupe glass.

4. Twist the lemon peel while holding it above the glass.

5. Drop the lemon twist into the cocktail for garnish.

recipe continues

☾ MAKING BLUEBERRY SYRUP:

✦ In a small saucepan over medium heat, combine 1 cup (240 ml) water, 1 cup (200 g) sugar, and ¼ cup (35 g) blueberries. Simmer for 10 minutes, continuously stirring in circles around the edge of the pot to dissolve the sugar. Let cool completely, then strain into a glass bottle or jar. Seal tightly and store in the fridge for up to 3 weeks.

Note

Any time you use a citrus peel, you should either rub it against the rim of your glass or hold it above your cocktail and give it a good twist. This allows the citrus peel's oils and aroma to be released, adding a refreshing fragrance to your cocktail.

Feel It All

★ ★ ★

So. Many. Feelings. And that's okay. This is a tasty mezcal cocktail that's light and pretty. Pür•likör has a great selection of other spirits that we love (blood orange and elderflower especially), but the pear has the perfect amount of fruitiness and sweetness.

GLASS TYPE

[COUPE]

INGREDIENTS

1½ ounces (45 ml) Banhez Mezcal Joven

1½ ounces (45 ml) Pür•likör Williams pear liqueur or other pear liqueur

½ ounce (15 ml) lemon juice

1 egg white

Lavender bitters

DIRECTIONS

1. Pour the Banhez Mezcal Joven, Pür•likör, and lemon juice into a cocktail shaker.

2. Add the egg white to the shaker.

3. First, do a dry shake (do not add any ice).

4. Add ice and shake again, vigorously.

5. Strain into a chilled coupe glass.

6. Garnish with a couple drops of lavender bitters.

Raw Egg Warning

Consuming raw or lightly cooked eggs poses a risk of food-borne illness.

Pisces Night Life

We can appreciate the emotional openness of a Pisces. Pisces, you can sometimes be easy to clock because your emotions are like a cute little pet Pomeranian: when you walk in the room with a Pomeranian, everyone notices it. This clarity also means that when you don't care for someone or something, you won't waste your time, energy, or mental real estate on it.

On weeknights at the bar, we see the entire spectrum of dates, and we can always spot a first date right away, from the awkward I-want-to-be-friendly-but-not-overstep-boundaries hug to questions about siblings and the go-to "What's your sign?" By the way, if someone has agreed to go on a date with you, you can probably go in for a quick hug when you meet them. We've seen enough hesitation hugs that turn into handshakes. Dates can definitely feel like job interviews sometimes (although some of us are looking for a different type of job), but you have our permission to drop the formalities and have some fun.

On one night, a man (date 1) walked into the bar solo and ordered a drink. He looked toward the door and his phone a couple times before another man (date 2) strolled through the door. They locked eyes and smiled at each other. Date 2 approached and the two looked at each other for a moment before one of them moved in for a hug. They sat down at the bar and started chatting, exchanging a few of those first-date pleasantries about where they're from and what their jobs are. Bartenders hear the craziest things, so trust us when we say we aren't purposely eavesdropping on conversations. They ordered a few rounds and it seemed like they were getting along. We were pleased—we love a good first date! We hope everyone gets along and gets laid and lives long, happy, fruitful lives. Then they started ordering shots—always a good sign that the chemistry is busting.

All of a sudden we heard a loud, "Wait, are you *joking*?" Date 1 had a confused look on his face while date 2 looked embarrassed. Date 1 says, "Please tell me you're joking." Date 2 says, "What do you mean?" Date 1, clearly annoyed: "We literally met at Unter [a popular local party] and fucked that night." Date 2: "Oh my god . . . wait, why didn't you say anything earlier?" Date 1: "I thought you knew and we were playing it cool!" Ladies and gentlemen, *that* is a start of a true Brooklyn romance.

So to all our Pisces, take some time once in a while and enjoy yourself. Not everything has to be the dramatic romantic trilogy of a lifetime. Sometimes you meet a cutie in the bathroom line at a foggy rave and just have a nice time and that's enough. Who knows? It might even turn into something more if you get out of your own way.

MERCURY IN RETROGRADE

We feel that it is important to add a couple of extra sections about significant moments in astrology. Although these are not sign-specific, they can dictate so much of your experience during the year and can explain irregularities in how you're feeling or how the world is just kicking you while you're down. Rude.

Mercury is the planet that rules communication and travel, and when the planet stations retrograde, many aspects of our day-to-day life become shrouded in chaos. If you wake up one day and your MacBook charger is broken, your new crush ghosts you, you spill a whole latte on your favorite pants, the WiFi is down, and you get fired from your job? Mercury might be stationed retrograde. There's not much to do at that point but let the tears fall—you've earned it.

Our recommendation for when Mercury Retrograde comes around is to plan for things to go wrong. Maybe hold off on signing that lease or buying that expensive air fryer. Our experience with it is to expect our dishwasher to break down or someone to punch a hole in our wall at the bar. But for those signs that thrive in chaos (looking at you, Aquarius), enjoy it while you can.

When Mercury stations retrograde, it can also be the magnifying glass that reveals the cracks in our lives that need to be patched up. Whether that's the dentist appointment you've been postponing for several years or a friendship that's run its course, the time has come to deal with your business. Look within yourself during this chaotic time for lessons to be learned.

♡ INNER LIFE, "I'm Caught Up
(In a One Night Love Affair)"

♡ SOLANGE, "Losing You"

♡ THE CHEMICAL BROTHERS, "Don't Think"

♡ PIXIES, "Wave of Mutilation"

♡ SKY FERREIRA, "Everything Is Embarrassing"

♡ JAMES BROWN, "Down And Out In New York City"
(feat. The J.B.'s)

♡ RADIOHEAD, "Weird Fishes/Arpeggi"

♡ SONIC YOUTH, "Incinerate"

♡ SOULWAX, "E Talking"

♡ 2 CHAINZ, "4 AM" (feat. Travis Scott)

OUR MERCURY-IN-RETROGRADE PLAYLIST

Fyre Festival

★ ★ ★

If you go to the bartender and say, "Just fuck me up," they'll probably give you something like a Long Island Iced Tea. Well, this is our version of that—just mix a bunch of different liquors and add some citrus, some sweetness, and a little color and you're on your way to a messy night. Good luck with this one.

GLASS TYPE

[HIGHBALL]

INGREDIENTS

½ ounce (15 ml) gin of your choice

½ ounce (15 ml) vodka of your choice

½ ounce (15 ml) tequila of your choice

½ ounce (15 ml) blue curaçao

½ ounce (15 ml) lime juice

Ginger beer

2 drops B'lure butterfly pea flower extract or grenadine

Lime wedge for garnish

recipe continues

DIRECTIONS

1. Pour the gin, vodka, tequila, blue curaçao, and lime juice into a cocktail shaker.

2. Add ice and shake vigorously.

3. Strain into a highball glass filled with ice.

4. Top off with ginger beer.

5. Add 2 drops pea flower extract, or ¼ ounce grenadine.

6. Garnish with the lime wedge.

Murphy's Law

★ ★ ★

One of the key ingredients to getting through Mercury Retrograde unscathed is learning how to sit patiently. It's like the violinist hitting those notes as the *Titanic* was sinking. Many of us feel the need to always jump on things quickly, but during these times we benefit from mulling it over first and acting with care. (Well, it didn't work out so well for the violinist, but at least he went out doing what he loved!) Here's a cocktail to help you slow down (and fall asleep, so you can save all this mess for tomorrow) before everything that can go wrong starts to.

GLASS TYPE

[ROCKS]

INGREDIENTS

1½ ounces (45 ml) Tito's vodka

1 ounce (30 ml) Giffard Rhubarb liqueur

½ ounce (15 ml) Dolin sweet vermouth

1 drop Peychaud's bitters

Rosemary sprig for garnish

DIRECTIONS

1. Pour the Tito's, Giffard Rhubarb, and Dolin into a mixing glass.

2. Add one drop of Peychaud's bitters.

3. Fill the mixing glass with ice and stir until all the contents are integrated.

4. Strain into a rocks glass filled with ice.

5. Garnish with the rosemary sprig.

SATURN RETURN

Another major astrological phenomenon is the Saturn Return. Much like Mercury Retrograde, Saturn Return has gotten a reputation for being a scary, tumultuous time, but this one specifically affects a person in their late twenties, specifically around ages twenty-seven to twenty-nine, and again in their sixties. It's said that during this stage in our lives, we may encounter many extreme challenges, upheavals, and wake-up calls. This can mean major shake-ups in your career, dating and relationships, familial stability, and friendships. Saturn is gonna give you some tough love, so during those real difficult times, just picture her like a fabulous auntie with tattooed eyebrows decked out in vintage Yohji Yamamoto as she tosses you into a pit of snakes like the little piece of coal that you are—and if you push through the turmoil, you'll come out on the other side as the shining diamond that you were always meant to be.

Sometimes we need to be pushed on what we accept as a given. And sometimes it's a gift to be able to step back and reevaluate the paths we have spent the last few years or longer trekking down, mistakenly thinking they're the only options we have. Yes, this period can be tough as hell, and then one day it starts to become easier. Whether it has to do with your love life, career, creative endeavors, or another major part of your day-to-day, just remember that there is no Hair-of-the-Dog trick to fixing this hangover. This is a great opportunity to test your patience and your ability to prevail. You'll wake up in your thirties more adept and confident than the day before, sipping on your favorite cocktail, living out the movies you used to watch.

♡ LCD SOUNDSYSTEM, "I Can Change"

♡ FISHMANS, "Long Season"

♡ MOODYMANN, "I'm Doing Fine"
(feat. Amp Dog Knight)

♡ SLOW PULP, "Idaho"

♡ JEREMIH, "Impatient" (feat. Ty Dolla $ign)

♡ HAKO YAMASAKI, "さすらい（Sasurai)"

♡ EARTH, WIND & FIRE, "Devotion"

♡ DON TOLIVER, "Can't Feel My Legs"

♡ NEW ORDER, "Ceremony"

♡ MINMI, "Who's Theme"

OUR SATURN-RETURN PLAYLIST

Meeting Dr. Melfi

When one era comes to an end and makes way for the next, it can feel bittersweet, whether it's Tony Soprano saying goodbye to all his ducks or you going through a tough breakup from someone you thought you would spend the rest of your life with. All you have to remember that era is a box of old Polaroids and a pair of someone else's old underwear. (Here's the hint you were waiting for to throw out your ex's Calvin Kleins.) The Meeting Dr. Melfi will accompany you through those tearful goodbyes because change is good . . . right?

GLASS TYPE

[ROCKS] OR
[WINE GLASS]

INGREDIENTS

1 ounce (30 ml) Del Maguey Vida mezcal

1 ounce (30 ml) Amaro Nonino

¼ ounce (8 ml) Campari

½ ounce (15 ml) passion-fruit nectar

½ ounce (15 ml) lemon juice

Fresh mint for garnish

DIRECTIONS

1. Pour the Del Maguey Vida, Amaro Nonino, Campari, passion-fruit nectar, and lemon juice into a cocktail shaker.

2. Add ice and shake vigorously.

3. Strain into a rocks glass or wine filled with ice.

4. Place a mint leaf on the palm of your hand and spank it to release the aroma, then drop it in the glass.

Goodbye, Dragon Inn

Named after a movie by Taiwanese director Tsai Ming-liang, which is one of the most beautiful and quiet films we've ever seen, this cocktail features Hendrick's, one of our preferred gins. We love its hints of juniper berries, citrus, and orange. American Fruits has a strong line of fruity liqueurs, and we love using black currant in our cocktails. Black currant looks like a little purple grape; flavor-wise it's tart and sweet, with wonderful notes of earthiness. The Luxardo adds a tint of bitterness that balances this cocktail out. Sip on this one. You deserve it.

GLASS TYPE	INGREDIENTS
[COUPE]	1½ ounces (45 ml) Hendrick's gin
	1 ounce (30 ml) American Fruits Black Currant Cordial
	½ ounce (15 ml) Luxardo Maraschino liqueur
	½ ounce (15 ml) lemon juice
	1 egg white
	Hibiscus flower for garnish

DIRECTIONS

1. Pour the Hendrick's, American Fruits, Luxardo, and lemon juice into a cocktail shaker.

2. Add the egg white to the shaker.

3. First, do a dry shake (do not add any ice).

4. Add ice and shake again, vigorously.

5. Strain into a chilled coupe glass.

6. Garnish with the hibiscus flower.

Raw Egg Warning

Consuming raw or lightly cooked eggs poses a risk of food-borne illness.

Editor: Shannon Kelly
Designer: Heesang Lee
Managing Editor: Glenn Ramirez
Production Manager: Sarah Masterson Hally

Library of Congress Control Number: 2021946852

ISBN: 978-1-4197-5889-8
eISBN: 978-1-64700-553-5

ABRAMS The Art of Books
195 Broadway, New York, NY 10007
abramsbooks.com